823BRO
c

PLAN of PART
of HAWORTH

1 Parsonage Museum
2 Sunday School
3 Church
4 Black Bull

D1613087

C

911

920 BRO

T10378

18-10

HAWORTH OF THE BRONTËS

by

PHYLLIS BENTLEY and JOHN OGDEN

TERENCE DALTON LIMITED
LAVENHAM . SUFFOLK
1977

Published by
TERENCE DALTON LIMITED
ISBN 0 900963 75 1

Text photoset in 11pt. Baskerville

Printed in Great Britain at
THE LAVENHAM PRESS LIMITED
LAVENHAM . SUFFOLK

Contents

Index of Illustrations

All illustrations, unless otherwise stated, by John Ogden.

Acknowledgements

We would like to acknowledge the help given to us by the following people in preparing the manuscript of this book: — Mr Ian Dewhirst, Reference Librarian, Keighley Public Libraries; Mr Derek Bridge, Reference Librarian, Calderdale Public Libraries; Mr Roy Tomlinson and Staff, Percival Whitley College Library, Halifax; Mr Norman Raistrick, Curator, Brontë Parsonage Museum, Haworth; Mr Leonard Kersley for the truly Brontë scene used on the jacket; and Messrs Douglas Ward and David Steel, Department of Art and Design, Percival Whitley College.

The three sisters, painted by Branwell. Reading from left to right they are
Anne, Emily Jane and Charlotte. *Brontë Parsonage Museum*

CHAPTER ONE

Haworth

The West Riding of Yorkshire — strangers — place of
Haworth — character — life in Haworth

THE forces of nature, with infinite patience and inexorable
power, have built up a range of hills in Yorkshire that are
often, and for good reason, called the backbone of England.
We know them now by the slightly grandiose name of the
Pennine Chain.

During the millions of years of its existence, this Pennine
part of our land had undergone the most amazing and
powerful changes. At one time a series of gigantic petrified
ripples in southern Europe corrugated the Yorkshire land into
the form we see now. Thus today the Pennines are a range of
hills which stretch from the borders of Scotland southwards
into Derbyshire. Broad in mass, they form a single geological
unit, though they vary in type and origin from place to place.
In the West Riding, at their base, lies a subterranean layer of
limestone; above this, interleaved shale and sandstone are
topped by grits (millstone grit), all of which occasionally
outcrop above the surface by reason of the tilts of the strata. A
deep layer of peat in some places tops all, while coal measures
which once covered all the Pennines, after countless years of
exposure to the elements are now reduced to lower patches
stretching towards the east. The land is not fertile arable or
grazing country, but hardy grasses, cotton grass, bents and
heather can flourish, birch trees survive, and dense stands of
oak which once choked the valleys still leave a few windblown
trees.

To the casual observer the Chain may well appear to be a
complex jumble as a result of its many diverging slopes and
valleys. Glance at a list of Yorkshire heights above sea level and
you will be astonished by the sudden swift neighbouring
variations. All Pennine roads go up and down, up and down, it
seems interminably, with only a short level strip (if any)
between.

The county of Yorkshire has a marvellous water-table, due
to the behaviour of the weather on the other side of the
Atlantic. Cold, dry polar air sweeps down from the Arctic
Circle across the vastness of North America. At the same time
another great air mass, hot and moist, wells up from the

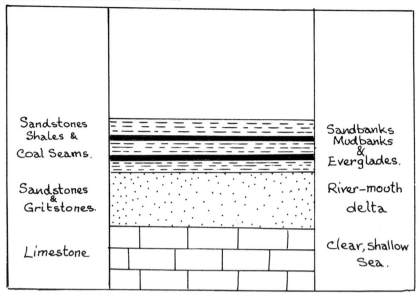

Sandstones Shales & Coal Seams. | Sandbanks Mudbanks & Everglades.

Sandstones & Gritstones. | River-mouth delta

Limestone | Clear, shallow Sea.

The origins of carboniferous Rocks.

The structure of the Pennines.

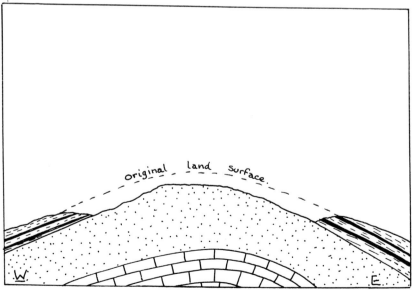

tropical seas of the Caribbean and Central America. Somewhere off the east coast of the United States the battle between the two is joined. Chilled by the polar air, the wedges and pockets of tropical air give up their water vapour and huge banks of clouds form, heavy with moisture. As the earth turns, these masses are drawn north-eastward and often burst in lashing downpours of rain upon the higher parts of the British Isles.

Hence there are nine main rivers in Yorkshire: Tees, Swale, Ure, Nidd, Wharfe, Aire, Calder, Derwent and Don. Seven of these flow south-east from the Pennines, joining others on their way. They come together mostly in the broad river Ouse, flow on south-east into the Humber estuary, and finally roll out into the North Sea. (It is not sufficiently recognised that the Humber drains far more water into the sea than any other English estuary.) These rivers are fed by hundreds of small, rapid, rocky "becks" as we call them, which are dear to all West Riding hearts; they continually erode and steepen the hillsides, facing east, down which they rush.

Besides offering great beauty and joyous sound, these becks are also one important source of West Riding prosperity, for they provide one of the great requirements of the wool textile trade: wool and water. We cannot understand Haworth and the Brontës unless we grasp what the wool textile trade means to the West Riding. What human being first introduced sheep to Yorkshire, who first in our county spun sheep's fleece into yarn and wove yarn into cloth, we do not know; but we do know that Charlemagne wrote to Offa, king of Mercia, in 796 A.D. asking that the wool cloaks should be sent in the future of the same breadth as in the olden time; that in the porch of the Parish Church in Halifax (our native town) is a stone engraving of a cropper's shears, a textile tool, dated by historians at about 1257; that in 1284, some 39 Yorkshire Abbeys were supplying wool to Flanders; that Earl de Lacy owned 3,000 sheep in Yorkshire in 1303. Hundreds of documents support the growth and prosperity of our textile trade ever since; in 1973, for instance, we exported 43.33 million square metres to the value of £92.08 million and during the first three quarters of 1976 some 33.16 million square metres worth £75.15 million went abroad. Sheep feed and have fed abundantly for hundreds of years on the rough grass and heather—they don't like heather much, I am told, but can live on it—while the water to wash the fleece, felt and scour the cloth, provide later the water power to drive simple machines, runs in innumerable streams down every fold of the hills. Soon the third requirement became, of course, the coal to make steam power to drive machinery, and this too the West Riding held beneath its soil.

This part of England, then, is a mass of hills, rocky, wild, cold, wet, unkind to cattle and to all crops save oats and occasionally barley. The summits of the hills are often flattish, peaty; some of them are covered in cotton grass and bents (tallish tough grass), with sudden small black peaty ponds showing brackish water. Other hills, those we natives strictly list as moorland, are covered in heather, gloriously purple in late summer, dark green at other times. The hillsides often stand deep in bracken; green in spring, richly brown in autumn, with long branched fronds, toughly herbaceous in stem, growing sometimes tall enough to cover the walker's head. Black rocks — but we may have a word to say later about their colour — protrude, tall, massive, agreeably sinister, here and there. A strong wind blows over all. Clouds, often grey and heavy, roll across the sky or fly rapidly; rain (or sleet or snow) is probable in season.

On the morning of Thursday, 20th April 1820, the Brontë family, that is the Reverend Patrick Brontë, his ailing wife Maria, née Branwell, and their six children, Maria, Elizabeth, Charlotte, Patrick Branwell, Emily Jane and Anne, journeyed from Mr Brontë's previous parish in the little West Riding village of Thornton to his new parish of Haworth. This environment was to be the main habitation and influence of their lives.

Strangers

This family with the strange name — who and what were they? How and why were they in the West Riding of Yorkshire, approaching Haworth?

Patrick Brontë was born in County Down, North Ireland, in 1777, the eldest of the ten children of Hugh Bronte, a Protestant farm labourer, and Eleanor (or Alice) his Catholic wife from the south of Ireland, who changed her religion on her marriage. It is sometimes said that Hugh's name was Bronte, sometimes Branty, sometimes Brunty, sometimes Bruntee, sometimes even O'Prunty, but the perishing of certain parish registers has left the matter obscure. It is certain that the children were Irish on both sides and poor, living in the customary whitewashed cabin; it is also certain that Patrick was at one time a linen weaver, and always a clever, hard-working, ambitious boy. He became a village school teacher, then tutor to the sons of the neighbouring minister, who — a disciple of John Wesley — encouraged the lad to become a Sizar (scholarship holder with some rather lowly duties) in St John's College, Cambridge. From that time onwards Patrick's name became Brontë; but whether this was due to the Registrar's poor spelling, to Patrick's Irish accent, or to the fact that Lord Nelson had just been created Duke of Brontë, we do not know. Let us give Patrick the benefit of the doubt, and be grateful to him for providing his children with such an agreeable and distinctive surname. At first, too, he signed himself Bronte, then Bronté; not until he arrives at Haworth do we find him signing as Brontë.

He took his degree in 1805, was ordained in 1806 and held curacies in Essex, then in Shropshire, and then, perhaps by the recommendation of a friend there, the Reverend William Morgan, in Yorkshire at Dewsbury, later at Hartshead.

While there he published (locally, in Halifax) a volume called *Cottage Poems*. Mr Morgan then introduced Patrick to Mr John Fennell, the headmaster of the Woodhouse Grove School near Bradford, an institution originally founded for the education of sons of Wesleyan ministers. After a couple of years Mr Fennell was ordained a clergyman of the Church of England. Mr Morgan was engaged to the Fennells' daughter, Jane. Mr Brontë conducted the first theological examination of the Woodhouse boys, and became a welcome intimate of the family.

Paying a visit to her uncle Fennell at this time was a young lady from Cornwall, Miss Maria Branwell. Her father, recently deceased, had been a councillor of Penzance corporation, one of her brothers was Mayor of Penzance. Mr Brontë and Miss Branwell fell in love, and a double marriage, Brontë-Branwell, Morgan-Fennell, took place in 1812. The school and the parlour where the courtship took place still exist.

Maria Branwell was a particularly sweet and lovable person; small, neat, always dressed very plainly but in perfect taste. She wrote the most delightful letters to Mr Brontë during their engagement. Her future husband kept these letters and gave them later to Charlotte, so we can see for ourselves that Maria

Maria Branwell (Mrs Brontë). "A very small antiquated little lady", according to Ellen Nussey.   *Brontë Parsonage Museum*

had a cultivated mind—the Branwells were Wesleyans and believed in self-culture—a sense of humour and an ability for fluent expression. She also wrote, and Mr Brontë kept, a piece intended for a periodical publication, on *The Advantages of Poverty in Religious Concerns*, much less charming, but correct to the heavily pious style of the day.

The marriage was happy; Mr Brontë became curate at Thornton, a rather quiet village not too far away from Bradford, and the young couple made good friends and lived a pleasant social life there. Mrs Brontë had children; her husband produced another volume of poems, two "novels", and several articles.

It is clear that Mr and Mrs Brontë were what the West Riding calls "off-comed-uns", that is, persons not native, born outside the speaker's place. The phrase is still in use, and not perhaps as jokingly as one might expect. It was used to me in talk by a young journalist from Bradford (about himself) only the other day. Mr and Mrs Brontë, though they came from different regions, were both Celtic in origin, and they had all the vivacity, the fluency, the vivid turns of speech, native to the Celtic race. Also they were both, in attempt at least, writers. Patrick had actually had books published. Clever, of course, but rather soft work for a man, in Haworth's opinion.

Characters less resembling the natives of Haworth than Mr and Mrs Brontë would be hard to find. Also Haworth was unknown to all except Mr Brontë, who as it chanced had a few months' acquaintance with his new home. What would Haworth be and do to them?

The Place of Haworth

Haworth, a village four miles south-west of the town of Keighley in the West Riding of Yorkshire, is not mentioned in Domesday Book (1089). It first appears as *Haveworth* in 1209. By 1381 it is written as *Haweworth*. A possible derivation of its name is from old-English *haga*, meaning a hedge or enclosure, and the possible origin of this name would seem to be an enclosure made with a hedge. Haworth shows all the West Riding characteristics we have mentioned.

It lies in the heart of the Pennine Chain, one part rising diagonally up the side of a steepish slope, at the top of which lie the buildings in which the Brontës were chiefly interested. The houses of another part of the village cluster round the lower slopes of a hill, known as The Brow, facing the main slope across the valley.

In this valley, to the south-east of the main hill, flows the

Perched on a hillside above the Bridgehouse Beck is old Haworth. This view from the south-east was drawn in 1912.   *From "A Springtime Saunter"*

Bridgehouse Beck, with its small tributaries. On the north of the first-mentioned hill, in its own valley, flows the Worth stream, with some small tributaries. This river has in fact been named in fairly recent centuries, and may possibly draw its name from the enclosure or holding, rather than the other way round. The point to remember is that the name of the village is nowadays pronounced How-earth.

These two streams, Bridgehouse and Worth, join to the north-west beyond Haworth and proceed together, as the River Worth, through Keighley, where they join the sizeable River Aire. Thus the two streams as it were enclose the main Haworth hillside in two sides of a triangle.

The third side of the triangle, above the main Haworth slope, is formed by a great stretch of moorland, which rolls away for miles to the border of the neighbouring county of Lancashire. This is true heather moorland. "Lonely, heathery Haworth" is a phrase often used by nineteenth century walkers who, interested in the Brontës, in their native county, or in the wild scenery offered by such striking outcrops as Ponden Kirk, recorded their observations in newspapers or illustrated booklets.

Any map with Haworth at its centre must show West Riding

textile towns at its edges. Keighley stands to the north-east, four miles away. Due east comes Bradford, 11 miles, and to the east lies Leeds about nine miles further. To the south-east comes Halifax 10 miles, with Huddersfield beyond, eight miles. South by south-west lies Hebden Bridge, not quite a town, but more than a village, eight miles.

Two villages nearer to Haworth must also be mentioned. Stanbury on the road to Colne and Lancashire, about two miles beyond the top of the main Haworth hill, and Oxenhope in the Bridgehouse Beck valley, slightly south-west, about two miles.

All these are textile places, though Keighley has also a considerable engineering industry.

The Haworth Society's admirable booklet on Oxenhope shows with perfect clarity that Oxenhope was a worsted weaving community in the nineteenth century. Haworth was the same, also Halifax. The census figures for Oxenhope give the men's occupation over and over again as woolcomber, worsted weaver, worsted spinner/manufacturer. (The others were farmers.)

A brief explanation of the difference between woollen cloth and worsted cloth may be useful.

Fleece for use in woollen cloth is carded (between two tools rather like hairbrushes), spun into a single thread on hand or wheel (by women usually in former days), woven into a coherent piece of cloth then "fuzzed up" by sharp-pointed teazle heads fastened in rows on wooden handles; the fuzz is then cut off by "croppers" with shears — a process of extreme skill — damped and dried in the fields on "tenters", long wooden upright frames like fences, The idea is that this "teasing" or "fuzzing" causes all the curly fibres of the wool to link tightly together.

For worsted yarns the purpose is different, namely to make all the fleece fibres lie straight and single, their curliness entirely subdued. The fleece is "combed". Usually two or four men sit or stand around a central stove heated by charcoal, to which the strands of wool are attached. Each man draws out a long strand and holding its end in one hand draws a heated pronged comb through it with the other hand. The heat of the charcoal, the draught from the cottage or mill windows necessary to preserve a reasonable temperature, the hard physical labour, the skill, make wool combing an unhealthy, but compared with other industrial occupations in the nineteenth century well-paid, occupation.

The yarn thus combed was woven into smooth worsted cloth. In 1810 Haworth ranked next to Bradford, and before Leeds and Halifax, in the amount of wool used in the worsted trade. By 1838 there were 600 worsted handlooms in Oxenhope, and 1,200 in Haworth. Looms run by power, water or later steam were introduced in the 1830's, but were not general till 1850.

It was not, therefore, actually in Haworth or its very near neighbourhood that croppers were employed, for they functioned in the *woollen* cloth manufacture. The revolt of the croppers against the introduction of cropping "frames" run by water-power, displacing the skilled men and leading to the formation of bands of "Luddites", their attack on a woollen mill and eventually the murder of a manufacturer, did not occur in Haworth. These activities took place in other local textile districts, notably the outskirts of Huddersfield, Halifax and Hightown in the Spen Valley, near Mr Brontë's lodging while he was curate in Hartshead (1812).

From Hartshead and the Spen Valley in general it is 16 miles. From Keighley, a long slow rise to Crossroads, then turn

The formidable hill of Main Street, Haworth, photographed in the 1970's.

right into a slow mild descent into the Worth Valley. After a couple of miles cross the river by the bridge, tackle a short distance of very steep hill, turn right and attack the long steep Main Street, which rises from 550 to 800 feet in half a mile. This is well paved with largish slabs of millstone grit, placed endwise as Mrs Gaskell tells us in order to give the horses' feet some purchase. Neither very wide nor very narrow, the street is lined by narrow causeways and shops and houses built close to these causeways. To walk it is quite hard work but West Riding natives are used to hills; cycling up is impossible; I have not tried horse transport; motoring is not too bad, if one does not meet a flock of sheep, a few prams, or some Haworth natives about their daily tasks — but then one usually does. At the top of Main Street, on the left, stands the *Black Bull* inn, of which we shall hear much; steps to the left lead to the church; in the Brontës' days a pair of stocks stood in this corner and still stand today; a lane to the left a little beyond leads up to the Parsonage, which stands at right angles to this lane looking down directly at the church. A path beyond through a stile takes us to the moors. The Parsonage, a good agreeable eighteenth century house built in 1782, gazes across a small garden to the graveyard, where gravestones both horizontal and vertical are to be seen in considerable numbers. In the Brontës' day their home had five good plain windows of agreeable dimensions in the second storey, four windows of similar size on the ground floor, and a central doorway with a dignified triangular pediment.

From Bradford and Leeds one travels, by good roads of slightly easier contours because these places are not so closely embosomed in Pennines, to the Crossroads, and then proceeds as before.

From Halifax one must take a long rise out of town up steep hills with occasional calmer stretches between, then turn left and cross a wild stretch of open land, grassy, extremely windy, much dreaded by all who have to attempt it in bleak weather. On reaching the Crossroads, turn left and proceed as before. Be careful, however, to bear right shortly in order to keep to the Worth Valley, or you will find yourself panting up a very steep road over Brow Moor, or if a mile or two further on, climbing up Cock Hill Moor to reach Hebden Bridge.

The Hebden Bridge route is far the finest way to reach Haworth. It has always been popular with walkers of spirit — I have often walked it in company myself, having secured transport for the seven miles from Halifax along Calderdale to Hebden Bridge. Cock Hill Moor (1,450 feet) is not a heather moor; its growth is the rough tallish grass called bents, cotton grass, and bilberries. Two or three fine reservoirs are harboured there, black peaty ponds occasionally occur; the wind is really fierce; one sees there the stone "stoops", the upright two-foot stones to guide the wayfarer and so plaintively lamented by Mr Lockwood in *Wuthering Heights*, when traces of their existence had vanished, obscured by a heavy snowfall. They are blackened at the top by industrial dirt, so as to show clearly against snow, and used to be whitened at the bottom to stand out against the rough grass. The Cock Hill Moor gradients are considerable. At last one drops into Oxenhope, comes to fields edged with the drystone unmortared walls common to the district, crosses the valley, climbs a short mild hill, turns to the right along an almost level road and finds oneself at the bottom of Main Street in Haworth.

Readers may express surprise that the mileages mentioned are so comparatively short. The miles are not long, but they are Pennine miles. Enough of their gradients has been said, I think, to show that they are not easily negotiable.

The Character of Haworth

By the fourteenth century Haworth has a chapel, as part of the Parish of Bradford, and by the next century this chapel has "glassen wyndowes" as the gift of a Haworth native.

Through the next centuries, though it was not involved in the major violent incidents of English history, it went on the

The true size of their fantasy world publications can be judged against a ten penny piece.   *Brontë Parsonage Museum*

usual quiet way, establishing a free school in 1635, preserving its church registers from 1645, its natives giving lands to establish rents for the income of the ministers—note this, we shall meet the trustees of these estates in a Brontë row later. A severe drought led to a fire on the moors, but native benefactors provided good blue clothes for ten poor children, and a church clock, in the eighteenth century.

Haworth did not, however, escape the religious problems of the sixteenth and seventeenth centuries. Unlike neighbouring Lancashire, where many families adhered to the old Catholic religion, the West Riding of Yorkshire had a strong, perhaps even a majority, inclination towards Protestantism and dissent. Indeed one could say they had a strong inclination towards rebellion in general; they had no liking for authority and this independence was much helped by their textile trade. They earned good money by their combing and weaving whatever the weather, paid their rent regularly with their earnings and felt beholden to no man. The Squire and his relations had not the great power and prestige they held in milder counties. A great many West Riding men fought on the Parliament side against Charles I under the Yorkshire hero Sir Thomas Fairfax. They submitted to Cromwell's rule at first with approval, later with some grumbling; we read of weddings being celebrated in the market place by magistrates. The Act of Uniformity in 1662 saw some ministers ejected from their livings, others resigning; history books commenting on the Conventicle Act of 1664 forbidding attendance at any meeting of four persons for worship except in a church, remark ominously that "the unrest in Yorkshire" made this necessary. Of course, the dissenting folk did not keep the law; they rode and walked hither and thither through rain, sleet or snow, held services in private houses, preached and prayed and escaped through the back windows when officers of the law approached.

This tradition was still strong in the next century, when the curacy of Haworth was held by the great William Grimshaw from 1742. This tremendous minister, who thought he had spent a soft week if he preached less than thirty times, was an ardent follower of Wesley, and gave himself entirely to the service of God. He sometimes rushed out from Haworth church in the middle of the service, and chased any man he found outside (in the *Black Bull*, for instance) into church by wielding a whip with no uncertain hand. His contemporaries thought he had a great civilising influence on the rough, tough, wild population of Haworth. But after two ministers had followed Grimshaw to the grave, a series of events arose in 1819 which make us wonder.

The Vicar of Bradford nominated the Reverend Patrick Brontë to the living. But the Trustees of the Church Estates refused to accept him because he was the nominee of the Vicar, whereas they believed they themselves had the right of nomination. Mr Brontë, then the minister at the neighbouring village of Thornton, declined to come without the consent of the parish. The Vicar of Bradford nominated the Reverend Samuel Redhead to the curacy. Thereupon the most frightful scenes occurred on three consecutive Sundays in Haworth Church. The story may be found in full in Mrs Gaskell's *Life of Charlotte Brontë* (Chapter II). To tell it briefly here; on the first Sunday of Mr Redhead's curacy a full congregation stamped in unison with their clogs and then clumped out; on the next Sunday a local half-wit rode irreverently into the church backwards upon a donkey; on the third a romp with a drunken chimney sweep and a bag of soot almost threatened the Reverend Redhead's life, but he escaped into the *Black Bull*. He gave up the living; Mr Brontë was appointed, the Trustees accepting him because they respected his earlier refusal. He managed the parish from February onwards while remaining in Thornton, and finally moved to Haworth with his family, as we have told, in April, 1820.

The natives of Haworth at this time, on their own showing, were still wild and rough. They were independent in defence of their rights; they bowed the knee to no man; they were stubbornly loyal to their own ideas, tending to look down on off-comed-uns; they believed they held the clean pride of doing all for themselves as opposed to the "mucky" pride of expecting others to do for them. They knew little of rank or birth, and scorned lofty airs or show-off; their speech was blunt, straightforward, strongly sardonic, rather slow, deriving its pith from dialect. They told few lies, but this was rather because they scorned their opponents than from a noble regard for the truth. They had a realistic view of money, which they valued, being honest and careful, but could be generous and hospitable when they liked. Glass windows and blue clothes for the poor were not beyond their ken, and later walkers in the district found shelter, warmth, cups of tea and lavish meals of ham and eggs heartily available. The custom of *arvills* at funerals, at which a handsome tea, or a glass of wine, with a pair of gloves or a funeral card, could be offered to sometimes as many as fifty or sixty people attending, is not mean or uncostly; it was strongly in vogue at this time. How would two Celts fare with such people?

Life in Haworth

The first impact of life in Haworth upon the Brontës was one of deep distress and disaster; for poor young Mrs Brontë, having given birth to six children in eight years, died of cancer in the autumn of 1821, exclaiming, it is said, as she lay dying: "My children! My poor children!" Few people need to be told what a serious gap, whether in body or spirit, the loss of a mother makes in a family. It was certainly so in Mrs Brontë's case.

If the Brontë children had not lost their mother while they were in infancy, aged from a few months to seven years old, it is most probable that they would not have experienced the severe isolation which marred, or made, their lives.

Mr Brontë did his best to repair his tragic loss. He asked a Thornton lady to marry him, but her heart was already engaged. He then proposed by letter to a young girl he had met in his first curacy in Essex, but it appears that he had courted her to a considerable extent and then left her in unmannerly fashion, for her reply to his proposal was one of burning resentment. After one more attempt he gave up the thought of marriage, and next year his wife's sister, Miss Elizabeth Branwell, came to live at Haworth Parsonage and take charge of its domestic affairs.

Of Aunt Branwell, as the children always called her, we shall have much to record presently. It is enough now to say that she was a very different person from her sister. Her income of £50 per annum was a welcome addition to the Parsonage funds, for she insisted on paying her share of the family expenses.

Perhaps this is the place to state that Mr Brontë's income was £200 a year. But as he pointed out in his ill-fated letter of proposal, he was "perpetual curate" of Haworth and nobody could take his curacy away from him; he inhabited for life a good solid house free of rent, and his income was derived from freehold estates, very solid and reliable. £200 in 1821 would be worth £800 or so in value in the early 1970's; but for a man with a family of six and, as they said in those days, "a position to keep up," ends had to be a good deal stretched to meet.

If we take a general look at the Brontë family at this point, our first impression is its isolation as regards transport. There was no railway service to Haworth in those days. Indeed the railway did not reach even as far as Keighley until 1847, when Charlotte was thirty-one. There was no bus or tram service. The Brontës could not, of course, afford to keep a horse. From Haworth one walked, over those Pennine miles; for special occasions one hired the local gig, for luggage one could employ the local carrier's cart. Papa and the children walked; Aunt Branwell rarely went out except to church.

When the Brontës first came to live in Haworth, in 1820, its population was about 4,600; in ten years it grew to over 5,000, and in another decade rose to 6,303. These figures include Oxenhope, Stanbury and outlying farms.

It is amazing how utterly unacquainted we are, through any direct words of the Brontë girls, with any individual persons living in Haworth. There are simply no records of social contacts. The children never seem to meet other children, never to play. Very few of the old landowning families still remained there. The new rising class of millowners doubtless had wives and children, at whose existence we may guess from the fictional pages of *Shirley*, but we do not meet them face to face. After all, there were at first six children at the Parsonage, enough to make their own amusements without outside help. They turned, we learn, rather to the moors than to Main Street, the six little things walking hand in hand across the moorland.

From what we read of the researches of Dr Mainwaring Holt, Medical Officer for Keighley in the 1940's, their avoidance of Main Street was just as well, for he gives (article in *Yorkshire Advertiser*, July 1947), an exceedingly disagreeable impression of sanitation in Haworth in the early nineteenth century. I quote from his record:

> "There was no public water supply in Haworth until private enterprise built a small reservoir which supplied water to thirty or forty houses at a charge of a few shillings a year. The majority of the villagers depended on pumps and wells . . . In order to have water for Monday's

washing, the poorer people were in the habit of going to a slowly running stream at two or three o'clock the same morning to fill their buckets. Drinking water was stored in stone jars. All the natural water supplies were more or less contaminated . . . Some houses built into the side of the hill were backless, and from them refuse was thrown into an open channel which ran down the street. There were no sewers in Haworth and most of the drainage ran in open channels and gutters . . . Uncovered midden heaps received household refuse, offal from slaughter houses and occasionally the drainage from pigsties . . ."

Another sanitation aspect of Haworth was also deplorable. The situation of the graveyard, at the top of the hill and only a few yards from the Parsonage windows, was not a healthy one from either village or Parsonage point of view. Dr Holt notes, too, that in the Brontës' days there was no public lighting in Haworth, though a few shops installed gas supplied by a local mill.

After the loss of their mother, the next event in the Brontës' lives was also one of loss, grief and further deprivation. The Reverend William Carus Wilson, a wealthy and charitable clergyman living in Westmoreland, founded a boarding-school in the little cluster of houses called Cowan Bridge, for the daughters of clergymen. The small fees paid by the clergy were to be supplemented by charitable subscriptions. Mr Brontë gladly took advantage of this opportunity for the education of his daughters, and the eldest two, Maria and Elizabeth, were sent there in the summer of 1824. Next month, August, Charlotte was also admitted, and Emily in November.

What the children suffered at Cowan Bridge has been recorded by Charlotte with intense bitterness in *Jane Eyre*. She may perhaps, as she hinted later to Mrs Gaskell, have regretted that she was perhaps a little less than just. But the result was that first Maria, and then Elizabeth, sickened, had to be brought home, and died in 1825 — probably from tuberculosis. Mr Brontë then, alarmed, fetched Charlotte and Emily home to Haworth.

Of Elizabeth we know almost nothing. But Maria was a gentle, charming, intelligent child, who could discuss all the politics of the day with her father, and replaced the fond care of her mother towards the younger members of the family. To lose her was terrible. Branwell seems to have felt her loss the most, for he wrote poems later to and about Maria, but Charlotte also mentions her with love. Maria's duties fell upon Charlotte, who accepted them with full love and responsibility. Maria was perhaps the most like her mother, the most sociable, the most easy in society, of the family; her loss increased their isolation.

In that year, 1825, however, two events occurred which tended slightly to lessen this isolation.

The first was the coming to the Parsonage of Tabitha Aykroyd. Tabby, as the Brontës always called her, was a native of Haworth, a strong, hearty, determined widow in middle life, who served in the Parsonage kitchen faithfully for thirty years. The Brontë children were her life; she cherished them, fed them, in early years accompanied them on their walks, kept them spotlessly clean, spoke sharply to them when she thought they deserved it — "you childer are mad" — but admired and loved them with all her heart. She had relatives living in Haworth, knew all the local personal history of past and present times, and could sometimes be coaxed or cozened into telling some of these tales, providing thus a connection between the children and the Haworth world as well as a solid foundation to their home life.

The other event was the foundation of the Keighley Mechanics' Institute, "establishing a library for the same". At the end of the first year, the Institute had 71 members and 150 volumes in the library. By 1831, when Charlotte was fifteen, the Institute had more than 100 members and more than 500 volumes.

Mr Brontë, it seems from the Mechanics' minutes, did not become a member until 1833, being number 213, but the fact that he was "billed" for a book by the Institute in April 1831 renders his admission date rather obscure. The Institute rules were strict, and a member was allowed to borrow only one single volume at a time (four if part of a set), though fines for late return of volumes were remitted for members living more than two miles distant. (Haworth was four miles away.) But it is perplexing to note that the Mechanics' Library was open for returns and withdrawals of books only on Monday and Friday evenings, from 8-10 p.m. I cannot believe that the young Brontës were allowed to walk those lonely four miles often on dark nights. Unless the Brontës had some other access to the Institute Library I cannot see how Charlotte had managed to read such an enormous amount before she began to receive a formal education at Miss Wooler's school at Roe Head in 1831. One of her schoolfellows, Mary Taylor, relates how the other girls at first thought Charlotte ignorant, because she knew no grammar and very little geography, but on the other hand soon found she knew a great deal about other matters — poetry, for example, and painting. Mr Brontë had not the money to buy many books. No doubt he and his wife had bought what they could. Perhaps Mr Brontë borrowed through other clerics? Perhaps Branwell (P.B. like his father) borrowed somehow? Or has another solution been found by Mr Ian Dewhirst, present head of the Keighley Public Library Reference department, in his recent gazetteer research? For in Edward Baines' *History, Directory and Gazetteer, Volume I,* published in 1823, he has found under *Booksellers* the entry "Aked, Robert (printer and circulating library)" in a Keighley street. Commercial circulating libraries are not much given to volumes of poetry and biography, it is true. But Robert Aked printed a monthly Sunday School periodical called *The Monthly Teacher*, which was edited by the Reverend Theodore Dury, Rector of Keighley, a friend of Mr Brontë, and host to the girls when they visited Keighley one evening to hear William Weightman's lecture. Perhaps Mr Aked provided some desirable reading for the Parsonage. Or perhaps Mr Dury borrowed for them from the Mechanics? But this was not really allowed.

Probably the largest and best source of books for the Brontës was Ponden Hall, Elizabethan mansion of an ancient family just outside Haworth, from whose library the children were allowed to borrow freely. Here were standard works, poetry, plays, essays. Two newspapers a week, and *Blackwood's* magazine, for which they subscribed, gave them plenty to read.

The most important event of the next few years for the Brontës, however, was one which, though it may not derive directly from the nature of Haworth, was undoubtedly encouraged by its isolation. Charlotte has given us, and Mrs Gaskell her biographer faithfully repeats, how the Brontës' daydream worlds and presently their childhood writings, began.

One winter's night the four children are sitting round the kitchen fire and are bored because Tabby refuses to light a candle for them. Branwell drawls lazily: "I don't know what to do."

"Wha ya may go t'bed," says Tabby in the comfortable but stubborn Yorkshire speech.

"Oh! suppose we had each an island of our own," laments Charlotte.

Each child now proceeds to choose an island for itself, and then goes on to people it with celebrated persons of the day, culled, of course, from their reading of Papa's newspapers.

The islands continue and develop; they have histories, become plays, in which the children collaborate in pairs: Charlotte and Branwell, Emily and Anne. Soon the Brontë children are writing, in tiny script in tiny home-made booklets measuring about 1½ by 2 inches (3 by 5 cms) the stories of these imaginary beings. The practice was given impetus when Mr Brontë brought home a box of wooden soldiers for Branwell; each child chose and named a soldier for their own, and the daydream stories proliferated. The little booklets were stitched, backed in shopkeeper's stiffish paper, given invented titles and authors' and publishers' names, all with great attention to real detail and much inventive power.

The stories began in Great Glass Town, an African kingdom ruled by Charlotte's hero the Duke of Wellington. Then presently Charlotte and Branwell decided to create another kingdom for the Duke's son. There was a great migration from Great Glass Town to the newly invented Angria, which this son, who became the Duke of Zamorna, ruled.

It was probably the scarcity of suitable paper in Haworth, as well as the scarcity of money to buy it, which led the Brontës at first to write in the very tiny hand they employed for these daydream stories. But later I think — this is my personal opinion only — they enjoyed the delightful format of their little books, which had all the apparatus of real large-size books in the real world. They may, too, have appreciated the privacy, the secrecy, which such tiny lettering gave their precious dreams, for the tiny books are quite difficult to read without a magnifying glass. This impression is strengthened by a full-sized exercise book presented to them by their father, which is inscribed:

> "All that is written in this book must be in a good, plain, legible hand."

One cannot but feel that he had caught sight of one of the

tiny books and disapproved of its minute writing. He was correct if he surmised that such script would be bad for the writer's eyes. This sizeable exercise book he gave his children is completely empty. Not a word is written in it. They would not write large as he wished, but were too scrupulous to use the book in a mode he had forbidden.

As I have said, the remoteness of Haworth did not *cause* these childhood writings. I have known children living in busy streets in lively townships who indulged in similar daydream constructions. We may, of course, surmise that all such children have vigorous imaginations, minds not fully occupied, and an inclination towards story-telling. But Haworth encouraged the children's continuance of these stories, because they had many empty hours to fill. We shall see later how their environment affected the content and style of these, as of all their other, writings.

Life at Haworth, then, went on quietly for the next six years. Mr Brontë walked his considerable parish, attended meetings, read newspapers bought and borrowed, taught Branwell (and perhaps little Anne) Latin, dined alone. Miss Branwell sat chiefly in her bedroom, which she shared with Anne; she read the newspapers, argued with her brother-in-law at tea-time when necessary, taught the girls good manners, ladylike habits and domestic skills.

Meanwhile Branwell skipped through his lessons with ease and occasionally accompanied his father round the parish; the girls did light domestic duties such as bedmaking, dusting, "brushing the carpet", peeling an occasional potato perhaps, and miles of sewing.

Unfortunately (probably) for himself, Branwell was not sent away to school. He might have been very unhappy at a public school—but then, so was Shelley, so was Winston Churchill. Mr Brontë had a Cambridge degree and taught his son himself. It is said that Branwell had a few terms' tuition at the Haworth School, but we may guess that he knew already far more than a Haworth school could teach him.

Fortunately, most fortunately, for the girls, Miss Margaret Wooler began with her sisters a boarding school for young ladies at Roe Head, a large comfortable house in Mirfield beside the Bradford-Huddersfield Road, twenty miles away from Haworth. Relatives of Mr and Mrs Brontë's Thornton friends, the Reverend Thomas Atkinson and his wife, who

were godparents to some of the Brontë children, offered to pay
for Charlotte to go to Miss Wooler's. She spent eighteen
months there as a pupil, later became a teacher there. Emily
followed and then Anne, as pupils.

This is really the first contact the Brontës had with the outer
world. It was contact with a school. All their contacts with the
outer world, except perhaps Emily's — but that we do not
know — were the schooling either given or received or both.

Miss Margaret Wooler was a delightful woman, a very great
contrast, not perhaps in nature but in the means of cultivating
it, with the people of Haworth. Small and stoutish, she yet had
an unforced dignity. Her dress was plain and simple, yet
tasteful, often white; her hair plaited into an imposing coronet.
She had a really sweet voice, knew French and Italian well —
she read a chapter of the Bible in Italian every day — and was a
born raconteur. She had a kind, amiable, affectionate dis-
position, fed her girls well, saw that they had plenty of outdoor
exercise but stood no nonsense and made them work hard. Roe
Head, only twenty miles, as I said, from Haworth, like most
West Riding houses stood on the slope of a hill. But the hill was
rolling deep green hillside above the coal measures, in the
shadow of the Pennines; no heather, no black rocks, much less
wind.

At Roe Head Charlotte made several important acquisitions,
which considerably affected her later life.

First, a solid base to her education. Perhaps we might add to
this a slight updating in dress and speech, Aunt Branwell's still
hearking back to the days of her Cornish youth.

Next, the idea of earning a living by teaching.

Then, the story of the Luddites — how they had met and
trained on the hill slope below Roe Head; how they had
attacked Rawfolds Mill and been beaten off. Miss Wooler told
this story vividly, and pointed out some of the scenes where its
actions had occurred.

Last, but by no means least for Charlotte, and of immense
importance to all readers interested in the Brontës: two
friends: Mary Taylor and Ellen Nussey. Each lived with her
family not many miles from Roe Head, though on opposite
hillsides of the Spen river.

It says much for Charlotte that these two friends differed so
strongly; they were different in politics, in religion, in tempera-
ment, in social standing. Ellen Nussey, fair, quiet, sensible,

intelligent but not at all intellectual, belonged chiefly to the landowning Conservative class; her uncle and great-uncle had been court-physicians, she lived in a house with battlements and an orchard, called Rydings. Her father was dead, her mother sensible and ordinary; she had brothers and sisters, some, as so often in families, a boon and some a bane. From the 1830's when she first met Charlotte till Charlotte's death in 1855, Ellen corresponded with Charlotte intimately and regularly and — this is so important it must be written in italics — *she kept all Charlotte's letters*, so that we can now read some four hundred of these invaluable documents. The girls visited each other's homes and stayed there.

Ellen's account of how she first saw Charlotte is famous; the silent, weeping, dark little figure with tightly curled hair and dark rusty-green stuff dress, who later proved to be near-sighted, unable to play games, but a model of high rectitude, close application and high abilities . . . no girl equal to her in Sunday lessons.

Ellen was acutely observant of surface details. In the Haworth Parsonage she found Mr Brontë venerable, courteous, almost handsome in his high white silk cravat, a superb raconteur. She notes his pistol, his dread of fire, his delight in the perusal of battle-scenes, his conducting of family worship each evening and winding of the clock on his way to bed. Miss Branwell's peculiarities, her front of auburn curls, her silk dresses and shawls, her gold snuff box, her clacking pattens, her continual talk of Penzance and dispraise of Haworth, Ellen notes with the mild respectful amusement often accorded to a friend's seniors. The pets — birds, cats and dogs — whom the Brontës loved so dearly, were not allowed by Aunt to be fed at table and in general were somewhat discountenanced by her. Ellen, whose manners were excellent and kindness reliable, concealed any comment too caustic, and was liked by everyone in the Parsonage, even by Emily.

Mary Taylor took a very different view of the Parsonage personalities. She saw through Mr Brontë, writing to Ellen later about his objections to Charlotte's marriage:

"I can never think without gloomy anger of Charlotte's sacrifices to the selfish old man."

But then, Mary belonged to a strongly Radical, strongly dissenting, manufacturing family, firmly entrenched in West Riding life for several generations, though financially distressed temporarily by the cessation of the Napoleonic wars, for the cloth the Taylor firm had provided for the British armies was no longer required. The Yorke family in *Shirley* are a pretty accurate picture of the real Taylors, as Mary herself admits:

"There is a strange feeling in reading it of hearing us all talking."

A very discreet hint in a letter from Charlotte to Ellen may indicate that Mary had a penchant for Branwell, which he perceiving then scorned. Mary was almost Charlotte's equal in intelligence, though devoid of true creative capacity, her superior in spirit. She went dauntlessly out to New Zealand, ran a successful shop there, wrote a novel called *Miss Miles*, took a Women's Lib attitude and upheld it with determination and good humour. On the deeper levels, Charlotte was closer to Mary than to Ellen.

A point to be noted here is that as soon as Charlotte emerged from Haworth she made lifelong friends. It was so also, to some extent, with Branwell, who in his painting studio in Bradford and later in his clerk's office in two small railway stations near Halifax (Sowerby Bridge and Luddenden Foot) made and retained friendships with the Leyland family and their literary and artistic circle. Joseph Bentley Leyland was a sculptor of some talent; in his youth his large statue of Spartacus, and later of a group of African bloodhounds, were well received.

Such friendships did not occur with Emily and Anne. Both sisters followed Charlotte to Miss Wooler's as pupils; Emily later taught for some months at Miss Patchett's boarding school on a hillside outside Halifax, and Anne was governess with two families. Anne's Robinson girl pupils respected her and came to see her in Haworth; but no friendships supervened. We cannot therefore blame Haworth entirely for their isolation. Emily, "a lightsome, graceful figure" in the 1830's, and "dear gentle Anne", in Ellen Nussey's words, were sufficient to each other.

CHAPTER TWO

What Haworth Meant to Each Brontë

Patrick — Elizabeth — Charlotte — Branwell —
Emily — Anne

W E HAVE been so long accustomed to speak and write of
the Brontës as a unit, that we are apt at times to forget
that the members of the famous family were individual
persons, with individual characters, temperaments and re-
actions. Thus, though they held some hereditary genes in
common — Irish and Cornish, with some Yorkshire environ-
mental influence superimposed in the girls' case — their
responses naturally varied. It is well worth while to consider
their responses to their surroundings separately before turning
to the influence of their surroundings on their writings.

The Reverend Patrick Brontë

The Reverend Patrick Brontë was, I think, fairly well
satisfied with his position at the head of the parish of Haworth.
He had risen several remarkable rungs up the ladder of class
then so difficult to climb. A poor farm labourer's poor linen
weaver son, in turn teacher at a small village school, tutor to
the vicar's sons, undergraduate at a famous Cambridge college,
university graduate, curate in Essex, in Shropshire and at
Hartshead, Thornton and Haworth in Yorkshire, theology
examiner at a prosperous Wesleyan boys' school, he now found
himself after some disagreeable opposition in which he behaved
admirably, "perpetual incumbent" of a Church of England
parish, monarch in a sense of all he surveyed. He accepted and
enjoyed this dominance without pressing it too far, for pressure
was not necessary.

He was married to a charming and loving woman, a
gentlewoman of the middle class by birth, and had six bright
children. He lived in a well-built house free; his stipend of
£200 a year was the equivalent of some £800 in the 1970's.
After his wife's death his sister-in-law, Aunt Branwell as the
children always called her, came to live at the Parsonage. She
was doubtless rather prosy, over-genteel and a bit of a bore,
but she was intelligent and could talk politics, taught his

children good manners and ran his household with some competence. Besides, she kept herself chiefly to her bedroom upstairs.

It must never be forgotten that Mr Brontë was an active parish priest, whom his parishioners respected. He was undoubtedly superior to all of them in culture and education. A university graduate, he had published a volume of poetry and two novels; he read newspapers and magazines, such as the famous *Blackwoods*, regularly. He preached often and by Haworth standards well, and did not hesitate to tackle contemporary happenings; when a bog burst, he traced the hand of God in it; he gave a fine obituary sermon on the death of his curate William Weightman.

He was not, in a word, as cut off from society and its normal usages, as his children. Ellen Nussey, for example, thought him a charming gentleman of the old school and a most interesting *raconteur*; his Irish accent was delightful and no doubt his parishioners enjoyed it.

He was used to living in the country and walked many miles with little fatigue and no fuss. Haworth was remote from towns, certainly, but so was his birthplace, Loughbrickland. No sentimental lover of landscape, he accepted heather and moor and black rocks in lieu of Ireland's green and pleasant land, without repining. He sat on committees, agitated about sewage and cemeteries, visited friends at Woodhouse Grove and Thornton and Bradford; we see him buying toy soldiers for Branwell in Leeds, a city where surely some clerical business must have taken him.

Though strict, he was a loving father; he took his meals alone in his study, but secured music and painting lessons for his children from neighbouring towns; this clearly required consultation and contact.

The process of turning a sheep's fleece into worsted yarn, requiring a laborious and difficult affair of "combing" — for as we said Haworth and the surrounding villages were worsted, not woollen weaving hamlets — is scarcely at all similar to the preparation of linen yarn from flax. I do not think Mr Brontë ever mentioned, either to his children or his parishioners, that he had been a weaver, but he surely could not feel that these villagers were completely alien to a man who had sat at the loom himself.

Mr Brontë was scrupulously honest and virtuous. Though

after his wife's death he made two, or perhaps even three, attempts to remarry, when these proved unsuccessful he resigned himself to an honourable celibacy and never spoke a flirtatious word. In his later life, there is just a hint that some parishioners smelled whiskey on his breath. Mr Brontë indignantly attributed this to the scent of eye-lotion. Who knows? In any case, no further scandal supervened.

For as a crowning favourable attribute, Mr Brontë liked to keep himself *to* himself, and this suited his parishioners, who often employed the phrase because they liked to do that too. In a word, they thought him "quite a one," and "not bad for an off-comed un," and he did not feel more strange than a parson should, in Haworth.

Elizabeth Branwell

To Aunt (Miss Elizabeth) Branwell, on the other hand, Haworth seemed the depth of barbarism. In her home town, Penzance, the climate, warmed by the Gulf Stream, was sufficiently mild to allow palms to grow out of doors and geraniums to flourish in winter; in Haworth the strong winds blew, rain, sleet and snow buffeted the house, the hills were unconscionably steep and badly paved. In Penzance her father was a respected tradesman, her brother Mayor of the town. Social life flourished, in which she had her own valued and decent position; tea parties abounded. In Haworth she had no woman friend, and probably spoke little to the female natives who are on record as saying that they never saw her except in church. She was an ardent, even an extreme, Methodist and despised the Church of England heartily, while attracted by some of its procedures. Some Methodist magazines of an extreme type, which she had brought with her or came to her, her false front of gingerish curls, the wooden pattens which she wore in the Parsonage because it was cold and draughty, her silk dresses, large caps and expensive shawls, were the subject of discreet but irritated ridicule to her nieces. But she was intelligent and for her day well read; she could talk politics to Papa admirably.

The old home in Penzance was broken up, and to be head of a parson's house was agreeable and would assist her to maintain a respectable front on her small income of £50 a year, but we must admit also that duty called Miss Branwell to Haworth, and Aunt Branwell was a great one for duty. She

Aunt (Elizabeth) Branwell. A high-principled Cornishwoman, she was out of her depths in the wilds of Yorkshire. *Brontë Parsonage Museum*

had loved her sister Maria, and Maria's children needed her. She was very fond of gentle Anne, who shared her bedroom, but Branwell was her favourite; we may ponder how far her Cranford-type gentility affected him. It seemed strange, perhaps, that her will divided her money amongst the three Brontë girls plus one Cornish niece and left only her "Japan dressing-box" to her nephew. This may imply that she had given Branwell money before, or merely that she expected a man to make his own way, but knew that three penniless girls had a hard time ahead of them. But in fact the dressing-case

was "my best Japaned dress-box," perhaps a heavily ornamented, prestige possession of stamped leather. We do not
know.

Aunt encouraged the girls in genteel feminine pursuits, as I
have said — the piano, drawing, sewing — but knew nothing of
their writings. I had thought that we never heard of her
entering the kitchen or taking any interest in cookery, but we
owe to Dr A. Rowse, the historian, a correction on this point.
He has deciphered some words in Emily's birthday note for
1834:

> "Anne and I have been peeling apples for Charlotte to
> make an apple pudding and for Aunt's . . . (Blur) Aunt
> has come into the kitchen just now."

The blur proves to be "nuts and apples" which Dr Rowse, a
Cornishman himself, describes as a then well-known Cornish
dish.

Aunt offered money to the girls to start a school, but the
project came to nothing, which was only too likely, thought
Aunt Branwell, in Haworth. If she thought herself something
of a martyr for staying in this cold, windy, lonely village, who
can blame her? She stayed in Haworth and did her duty, and
her rather too frequently expressed distaste for the place
probably confirmed the girls in their love for it. One good and
fine action Aunt performed: she found the money for the girls'
stay in Brussels.

Charlotte

There were two strands in Charlotte's feelings towards her
environment.

On the one hand, she had a passionate loyalty towards her
family and her home. "Our England is a bonny land, and
Yorkshire is one of her bonniest nooks", she says staunchly in
Shirley. She had, we are often told, a particular fondness for
observing the skies and the weather.

The deaths of her mother and two elder sisters had left
Charlotte to play their parts, to be as it were in charge of the
Brontë family. She was active and practical in care for them;
all those small but important details of food and clothes which
a mother supervises, fell to the loving care of Charlotte; we see
in her novels her constant observation of draughts, damp shoes
and shawls. In her letters to Ellen Nussey, Charlotte frequently
notices her sisters' health. Anne's cough is the subject of an

actual quarrel between Charlotte and Miss Wooler. "Here, Branwell, read this," said Mr Brontë to his son, handing him a letter, "and show it to your aunt and Charlotte." Mr Brontë consulted Charlotte; relied on the good sense and practical advice of his eldest remaining daughter.

Charlotte also played a not unimportant part in the affairs of Haworth parish. She taught in Sunday school, "headed a table" at the annual treat, was the day-school visitor and the needlework inspector. In these capacities she was considered very strict, especially with the children, enquiring scrupulously whether the garment under consideration was the child's own work, but praising generously when it proved to be so. She does not mention these duties in her letters, but accepts them without question, for Haworth was home to her.

On the other hand, we must not forget Jane Eyre's passionate outburst when Rochester, teasing, asks her if she is sorry to leave Thornfield.

"I love Thornfield — because I have lived in it a full and delightful life . . . I have not been buried with inferior minds, and excluded from every glimpse of communion with what is bright and energetic and high. I have talked, face to face, with what I reverence, what I delight in — with an original, a vigorous, an expanded mind."

In a word, Charlotte's longing for something beyond Haworth was entirely spiritual. She wanted to see great cities, hear great music, see great paintings, meet really great people, live on a high cultural plane. One can feel all this, and still love dear old Haworth; Charlotte did so. When she murmurs, "I want us all to get on," she is yearning for cultural improvement. When she reads Mary Taylor's account of travels abroad, we have this fully expressed. She cries from her heart in a letter to Ellen Nussey:

"I hardly know what swelled to my throat as I read her letter . . . such an urgent thirst to see — to know — to learn . . . I was tantalized with the consciousness of faculties unexercised . . . I so longed to increase my attainments to become something better than I am . . .

In extreme excitement she wrote a letter home which carried her point; she made an appeal to Aunt for assistance which was answered by consent, for Aunt agreed to lend the necessary money.

And so Charlotte and Emily were enabled in 1842 to go to

THE FOUNDLING

A TALE OF OUR OWN TIMES BY

CAPTAIN

TREE

Author of the Incorporeal watcher, the green Dwarf, The wise ort's ca ve. Alphonso Howard, a year of horrows, the Forgotten ring The ★ Pledge &c. &c.

PRINTED AND PUB.
LISHED
BY

SEARGEANT TREE HOTEL.
STRE ET
VERDOPOLIS

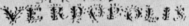

And by all other book sellers what-
so ever

Whether for the Duke of Wellington's Son
hy's Parryl or Ross's Glass Towns &c.&c.

THIS BOOK

Was begun May 31st 1833 and
finished June the 27th 1833

Charlotte

Brontë

The title page of *The Foundling*, dated 1833, and signed by Charlotte Brontë. This was one of the miniature books that the children produced.

Brontë Parsonage Museum

school in Brussels, and Charlotte met the great adventure of her life.

At Madam Heger's highly respectable and admirably con-ducted pensionnat de jeunes demoiselles, in Brussels, M. and Mme Heger had been favourably impressed by their letters of application; they saw at once that the Brontës — daughters of an English Clergyman — were serious persons, eager to learn so as to qualify themselves to earn their own living as teachers. They treated the girls well; M. Heger, who was "professor" at the boys' school next door and took only a few courses in his wife's school, gave special lessons on carefully arranged lines, to the two English girls, and did not, it seems, charge extra for them. He thought Emily had the finer mind of the two — though Emily did not agree with Monsieur very well. He encouraged them both to write essays of their own in French, and made comments in the margin which show a true feeling and understanding for the French language and French literature. Emily gave a few music lessons — not Charlotte; she declined a favourable governess post because she felt she had not the required musical skill; her pupils liked Emily and all went well.

But in October of 1842 the girls received a letter from home telling them that Aunt Branwell was very seriously ill, perhaps even dying. They left for Haworth at once, but were too late on the sad errand; when they reached home Aunt's death and funeral were over. The young Brontës felt a respectful regret for her demise, but not, I fear, any real or deep personal sorrow.

Meanwhile M. Heger had written a most courteous and amicable letter to Mr Brontë, praising the girls' ability and hard work, and urging that they should return to the school to complete their qualifications. Emily did not return; Charlotte, prompted by what then seemed an irresistible impulse which afterwards she bitterly regretted, returned to the Heger pensionnat in January and spent an increasingly unhappy twelve months there.

In letters to Ellen Nussey and even to Emily, Charlotte tells of her loneliness, her misery. After lesson-time she had nowhere to go save the empty garden or the cold empty class-rooms. The Hegers told her she must use their private sitting-room as her own, but of course she did not like to do so. M. Heger gave her very few lessons; she took a German course from another teacher and paid heavily for it. Her dislike of Mme Heger grew

The Heger family painted by Ange François in 1847. This portrait conveys a closer likeness of Monsieur Heger when he was known to Charlotte than those showing him in later life.

By permission of Monsieur René Pechère, Brussels

and grew. The climax of her misery was probably reached in September, when out of sheer loneliness the decidedly Protestant Charlotte actually presented herself at a confessional in a Catholic Church. "Better not tell Papa of this," warns Charlotte.

The truth was of course, that poor Charlotte had fallen in love with the first man of intellect she had met: M. Constantin Heger. The photographs usually inserted in books about Charlotte show him as an agreeable seventy. But the contemporary pictures of himself or with his family, reveal that he was in fact a distinguished looking man of thirty-three when he first met Charlotte — only six years older than she was. M. Heger was very much in love with his wife, and probably accustomed to pupils who tended to love though fear him, so he did not take much notice. But Mme Heger had perhaps a shrewder eye. At one point she would have accepted Charlotte's resignation if her husband had not prevented her; and when Charlotte at length in December 1843 decided to leave the pensionnat, she saw the girl off to the steamer for England with remarkable celerity.

Charlotte at home in the Parsonage from January 1844, was now qualified, she thought, to open a private school, and had some money (bequeathed by Aunt) with which to do so; also she longed passionately for some active stake in life, some work to do. But Papa was ill, and losing his sight; she could not leave him, so the school project must be abandoned. It is to this period that belong those letters which Mrs Gaskell so mercilessly censored; letters to M. Heger of the most sad, almost piteous, kind. It seems there was some arrangement with him that she should only write to him at stated intervals.

> "It is not my turn to write to you . . . Ah, Monsieur! I once wrote you a letter that was less than reasonable . . . For six months I have been waiting for a letter from Monsieur . . . if my master withdraws his friendship from me entirely I shall be altogether without hope . . ."

The girls made an attempt at founding a school in the Parsonage — they even had some circulars printed and passed them to their friends. But it was in vain; Haworth was too remote, too wild; they did not receive a single application for a pupil entry.

Arthur Bell Nicholls came to Haworth as Mr Brontë's curate in this year, 1845. But at this time the occurrence was of no particular interest to any of the Brontës.

The news which came was bad. Anne of her own decision, left her post as governess with the Robinson family at Thorp Green. Why, we are never quite certain: it may have been because the eldest Robinson girl, Lydia, eloped with an actor and Anne was blamed for not guarding her more carefully; or it may have been because of Branwell's behaviour with Mrs Robinson. Certainly the Reverend Mr Robinson (more a country squire than a parson) dismissed Branwell with contumely, describing his conduct as bad beyond expression.

From now onward Branwell became a running sore in the Brontë family.

But in this terrible year an event occurred which changed the whole course of the girls' lives. Charlotte came across a notebook full of Emily's poems. We will consider these, what Charlotte thought of them, what happened as a result, when we come to speak of all Emily's writings. Meanwhile let us see that life in Haworth, with short excursions to Roe Head and Brussels, had not deteriorated Charlotte's literary taste, her capacity for passion, or her realisation that she did not know enough about getting a book published to undertake it without assistance. She wrote to several publishers; most did not reply, but a letter to Messrs Chambers in Edinburgh brought forth advice, on which Charlotte acted.

Poems by Currer, Ellis and Acton Bell, the Brontës' pseudonyms, were published by Messrs Aylott and Jones in May 1846.

Branwell

Patrick Branwell Brontë was the Billy Liar of the age, one of those story-tellers who cannot resist adding a picturesque detail to the anecdote — of course an anecdote in his favour. He spoke well and fluently, profiting perhaps by conversation with his aunt, and enjoyed the sound of his own sweet and pleasant tones, so superior, he could not help observing, to the heavy Yorkshire utterance of Haworth. He was the boy for the bright lights, longing passionately for London. He would not stay long in Haworth, of course, he thought, for it offered no scope for his many brilliant talents, in painting, writing, music; meanwhile Bradford would do.

But interestingly enough Branwell was not a snob; he made more friends in Haworth than the rest of the family; we remember his letters to the sexton John Brown; we remember that Branwell played the organ, talked brilliantly to the *Black Bull* audience which loved him, became a member of the local branch of Freemasons and played the organ at their Christmas Day service. But he had that attraction, that inclination, so often felt by the naïve, towards the sophisticated and naughty. For my own part — it is a personal opinion — he was not nearly as sinful as he pretended. His sisters understood him with a loving smile; see how Charlotte, as she describes the emigration from Great Glass Town into Angria, narrates how Patrick Benjamin Wiggins (such telling initials; Wiggins was Branwell, of course) went into an inn and came out boasting of the beef and beer he had consumed, when those outside had seen him through the window consuming tea and bread and butter. In Branwell's early youth, when he was the admired hope of all his family, he was probably chaste and sober enough. Only after his failure in London did he despair and take to drink, debt and opium.

Why did he fail in London? Other young men who left narrow provincial homes to try their luck in art in the metropolis did not waste their resources in a rather low-life inn, chatting to pugilists, as he did. Some indeed, notably the son of the Leeds painter who taught the Brontës, actually succeeded. Branwell probably tells us the whole story in an extract from the adventures of his dream-world Angrian hero, Charles Wentworth, in the capital city of Verdopolis in Angria. As Wentworth after long intense anticipation beholds the great river whereon Verdopolis stands:

"His mind being overstrained the relapse was as strong as the spring . . . He entered his hotel, stretched himself on a sofa, and listlessly dreamed away his time till dark."

Next morning he gazes at the magnificent buildings of the city but does not enter them.

"He found the reason of his hesitation proceeded from instinctive fear of ending his pleasure by approaching reality . . . Next morning found him still unknown and unvisited . . . and with the same anxious face feeding his feeling 'with little squibs of rums.'"

Here indeed we have the secret of all Branwell's failure: his addiction to daydreams. The personages of Angria, for instance, Rogue who became Duke of Northengerland and King of Angria, with his army, his grandiloquence, his mistresses, occupied far too much of Branwell's time and affection. His sisters too, continually and persistently day-dreamed; Charlotte in Angria, Emily and Anne in Gondal. Why and how they liberated themselves sufficiently to confront real life, whereas Branwell did not, requires perhaps a careful modern psychiatric study. But it may simply be that there were three girls, so that *talk* sometimes occupied them; or that the girls, being nineteenth century girls, were continually confronted with the domestic problems of actuality—making beds, dusting, baking, sewing—with Aunt Branwell and Tabby in their respective spheres keeping them firmly to these duties;

while Branwell being a nineteenth century boy was excused all such female business, scampered through his lessons and was left with far too much time on his hands in which to visit Angria. And he was alone. It is said that he went to school in Haworth for one term, but it had little to teach the son of a Cambridge graduate; the boy had no friends of his own age or kind until he met the Halifax Leylands. Bentley Leyland was a minor sculptor but of some repute — a huge figure of his composition stood for many years in the entrance to the Halifax Municipal Library. To sit with the Leyland brothers round a table, smoking, drinking — not much, but more than Haworth Parsonage would approve — discussing art with someone who practised it, was Branwell's highest pleasure.

His aunt's disdain for Haworth perhaps sharpened his perceptions. He did not believe overmuch, probably, in Penzance gentility, but that thrust dear old Haworth even further down the scale. He was fond of Haworth, of course. Fonder than Charlotte was, undoubtedly, for being male he was free to wander through the village and did not feel as crunched and suppressed by it as his elder sister. But London, London was his aim.

Young men may go to the bad in town as well as country, but I cannot help feeling that the isolation of Haworth was a grave disadvantage to Branwell. Our own native town of Halifax (population about 93,000) is not a metropolis, but yet some three hundred amateur societies are listed in its local year-book. This means that whatever subject you are interested in — from canaries to chamber music, from history to yachting — there is always a group in the neighbourhood earnestly studying it. Young, active lively society might have drawn Branwell away from Angria.

Emily

It might be thought that Emily, if as we shall claim she was a great poet, a space-sweeping philosopher, familiar with the depths of human wickedness and the miseris of human weakness, would have been intolerably fretted by the narrow confines of Haworth. But in fact exactly the opposite was the case.

In her preface to the 1850 edition of *Wuthering Heights* Charlotte writes of Emily that she did not,

"describe as one whose eye and taste alone found pleasure

in the prospect; her native hills were far more to her than a mere spectacle; they were what she lived in, and by; as much as the wild birds, their tenants, or as the heather, their produce."

Charlotte's superb *Memoir to Emily* (1850) gives the true and deep explanation of this feeling:

"My sister Emily loved the moors . . . She found in their bleak solitude many and dear delights; and not the least and best loved was — liberty. Liberty was the breath of Emily's nostrils; without it, she perished."

Thus Emily was happy, content, satisfied, when she was at home alone in the Parsonage with her father, writing in one of these eighteen month periods twenty-one poems, but at Miss Wooler's and the Pensionnat Heger she had to exercise the most severe moral restraint and compulsion to force herself to her duty of learning. M. Heger perceived that Emily had the finer mind of the two sisters; Charlotte alone knew what absence from the moors cost her sister.

Anne

Dear, gentle Anne, as Ellen Nussey called her, lost her mother before she was two years old. She saw two loving elder sisters die when she was five. During the months of the absence of Charlotte and Emily at the Cowan Bridge school, Anne was at home in the Haworth Parsonage with her father and Aunt Branwell. While Charlotte and Emily were at Miss Wooler's, and later when they were in Brussels, Anne when at home was in the Haworth Parsonage with Aunt Branwell. Whenever she was at home, Anne shared Aunt Branwell's bedroom until Aunt's death when Anne was twenty-two. Aunt Branwell had been brought up as a strong Methodist, in the days before Wesley left the Church of England. It is not surprising, therefore, that in the comparative isolation of Haworth dear, gentle docile Anne fell naturally under the influence of her aunt, and took to herself unfortunately the darker side of some almost Calvinistic teaching, the feelings of sin and guilt which were then thought proper to inculcate in the tender minds of children. "My sister Anne," said Charlotte mournfully in *Biographical Notice of Ellis and Acton Bell*, 1850, after her death,

"was naturally a sensitive, reserved and dejected nature . . . long suffering, self-denying, reflective and intelligent, a

46

constitutional reserve and taciturnity placed and kept her in the shade, and covered her mind and especially her feelings, with a sort of nun-like veil, which was rarely lifted."

That Anne really loved religion, really loved the church, we see plainly in her plea, on the last Sunday of her life, in Scarborough, to be taken to the morning church service, so that she might share in the public service of God. By this date, it was 1849 and she was now twenty-nine years old, she had conquered to some extent the feelings of sin and guilt which had darkened her childhood.

For if the gentle Anne was partly shadowed by an Aunt of too Calvinistic tone, there was another side of her nature which bloomed under Emily's joy in life. Anne had not the passionate adoration, the intimate participation, of Emily for and in the moors — but with all the sweetness of her nature she loved the smaller forms of life which she could protect. She loved the flowers which bloomed there, blossoms small in themselves, growing close to the ground; the purple heather bells, the

Lonely, heathery, Haworth. A close-up of the local moors where peat, heather and gritstone boulders are gashed by a moorland beck as it drops from the level summit.

white clover, the strange blue of harebells, the yellow primrose. She loved the birds: lapwings with their excited angular flight, larks with their heavenly song, curlews with their deep lament; she loved the lambs, so pretty in their curly coats, so graceful in their gambols. She also, Charlotte tells us, loved the *distant* prospects of the moors; the hills sometimes blue, sometimes green, sometimes dark with rock, changing their colour as sun and cloud moved over them. The steep rough rocky climbs, lashed by the wind, were for Emily; the views toned down, romanticised, by distance were for Anne.

We must also note that Anne loved Haworth dearly, though not perhaps very perceptively, as the place where she was at home. From an agonising and brutal time in her first post to a different but acutely insolent form of depression with the Robinsons, when Emily spoke significantly of her as *"exiled and harassed* Anne", Haworth was to Anne what we all mean by Home.

Thus when Branwell's deterioration destroyed the peace of the Parsonage, Anne's poem *Domestic Peace* reveals the anguish felt by the gentle girl. Her last refuge seemed to be destroyed.

We must also remember that it was in Haworth that Anne met William Weightman, the brisk, lively, intelligent and kind young curate who came there in 1839. Charlotte is amusing and rather sarcastic about Weightman, whom she calls Celia Amelia and represents as rather flirtatious, warning Ellen Nussey against taking his advances too seriously. Whether Charlotte perceived Weightman's feelings for Anne we cannot tell from her joking account of him in church:

> "He sits opposite to Anne . . . sighing softly and looking out of the corners of his eyes to win her attention — and Anne is so quiet, her look so downcast — they are a picture . . ."

Of Anne's feelings for him, if any, it seems Charlotte had no real notion. Indeed Anne took pains to hide it. But we may perhaps see its effect when considering her poems.

CHAPTER THREE

Influence of Haworth on
Brontë Writings

Charlotte: novels and poems — Branwell: prose and poems —
Emily: novel and poems — Anne: novels and poems

Charlotte: Novels and Poems

BEFORE we turn to the effect of her environment on
Charlotte's writings, her four novels and her poetry, let us
consider for a moment her own definition of originality. It
occurs in *Arthuriana*, described as a miscellaneous collection
of pieces in prose and verse by Lord Charles A. F. Wellesley,
the son of that great Angrian the Duke of Wellington. The
Marquis of Douro, engaged in a cruel trick on an architect
who wishes to become a playwright, describes originality thus:

"It consists in raising from obscurity some theme, topic,
employment or existence, which has hitherto never been
thought of by the great mass of men, or thought of only to
be despised; in pouring around it the light of genius,
proving its claim to admiration by the subtle tools of logic,
clothing it with all the bright hues of a lively imagination . . ."

Douro's intention was, I fear, sardonic towards the un-
fortunate architect, but the definition is sound enough. This
kind of originality is exactly what Charlotte displays in her
novels: the despised teacher, the plain governess, the cloth
manufacturer and the working man smelling of dye, the
parson's unimpressive spinster niece—who thought of them as
suitable heroes and heroines till Charlotte raised them from
obscurity and clothed them in romance?

The Professor

Nothing in life was ever made easy to the Brontës. Each step
towards the success they presently achieved was made with
much anxiety, initial disappointment and suffering. Their
poems sold only two copies and the reviews were few and not
enthusiastic, though one spoke of Ellis Bell's "evident power of
wing". But young writers are immensely stimulated by the
sight of their own words in print; once print, actual print, has

been achieved they feel their feet are on one step, even if a low one, of the literary ladder. That is, they do this if they are in truth writers; the faint hearts may stuff the manuscripts away in a drawer and give up the idea, but those who really care go on.

The Brontës of course went on. We are not quite sure whether the three sisters were already writing their first real life novels, or whether they began to do so now. At any rate, Charlotte's *The Professor*, Emily's *Wuthering Heights* and Anne's *Agnes Grey* were soon ready to go to a publisher. These manuscripts were perseveringly obtruded upon various publishers for the space of a year and a half, Charlotte tells us; usually their fate was an ignominious and abrupt dismissal.

At last Emily's novel and Anne's were accepted by Messrs Newby, though on terms somewhat impoverishing to the authors. Perhaps this acceptance was because together they made up the three volumes then thought necessary for a novel. But Currer Bell's found acceptance nowhere, nor any acknowledgment of merit, so that something like the chill of despair began to invade Charlotte's heart. (It is right to mention that these parcels were often despatched to a new publisher with the previous publisher's address on the label just crossed out but left legible; a singular naïveté.) This was the year (1846) when Charlotte took Mr Brontë to Manchester to have the operation for cataract performed; it is said that she received the *Professor* script, rejected once again, that very afternoon.

The Professor is a very grim novel.

In a preface written later to the book in the hope of its publication after *Shirley*, Charlotte announces firmly and clearly her intentions. She explains how in many a crude early effort (Angrian) as we know, she had got over any such taste as she might have had for ornamented and redundant composition, and come to prefer what was plain and homely.

> "I said to myself that my hero should work his way through life as I had seen real living men work theirs — that he should never get a shilling he had not earned; that he should not even marry a beautiful girl or a lady of rank . . . As Adam's son he should share Adam's doom, and drain throughout life a mixed and moderate cup of enjoyment."

These intentions she carries out literally and faithfully. We must remember that this was a very black time for the

Brontës. Charlotte had returned, hopeless of her love, from Brussels the previous year; Anne had left the Robinsons of her own accord this summer; the school scheme had collapsed; Papa had cataract; Branwell had been dismissed. Not surprising that Charlotte's tale was grim.

It is, indeed, a very grim novel.

The tale opens in an industrial town in the north, where William Crimsworth, having been thrown off by his aristocratic uncles, seeks employment from his manufacturing brother, Edward. The scenery is that of a smoke-laden textile town. Edward Crimsworth is odious, the clerk with whom William shares an office is also odious in a subdued way; just to make life grimmer William's only friend is Yorke Hunsden, a man sarcastic and impertinent to the degree of insult. Hunsden, the Crimsworth mill and the town surrounding it are all very definitely nineteenth century Yorkshire, Aire Valley—not the Yorkshire we love but one whose existence we cannot honestly deny. However, Hunsden gives William a letter of introduction to an English merchant in Brussels, and he is soon off to Belgium.

Here too the tale is very grim. Installed as a teacher in the school of M. Pelet, Crimsworth soon grows to despise the surface courtesies of the Parisian, and when presently he is invited to give English lessons to the girls in Mlle Reuter's school next door, he discovers both her hypocrisy and the girls' brutality all too soon. Charlotte's description of the various

The Worth Valley looking downstream to the Aire Valley beyond. Rough, bent grass clothes the field in the foreground.

school girls with their Belgian titles and varnished hair is really atrocious, brutal and sarcastic though telling. The only "good" character in the whole story is Frances Evans Henri, daughter of an English mother and a Swiss father, brought up by an aunt in poverty, a lace-mender eager to learn, whom Crimsworth soon falls in love with and eventually achieves.

A recent study (*Myths of Power*, by Dr Terry Eagleton) purports to see in *The Professor* a thoroughly Marxist attitude on Charlotte's part to the various classes portrayed. That Charlotte shows a certain jealous resentment of the rich is partly true, but we must remind ourselves that it is the rich and uncultured whom she particularly dislikes, and unluckily this is the class whom she chiefly saw.

The awful moment of the rejection of *The Professor* by Smith and Elder turned out to be in fact, the turning point of Charlotte's life, for with the script came a letter—of two pages—stating that they were not disposed to publish the book, but also discussing its merits and demerits so courteously, in a spirit so rational and enlightened, that Charlotte took heart. While Mr Brontë lay upstairs in a darkened room, attended by a nurse, Charlotte downstairs began to write her second novel, *Jane Eyre*. She sent it off to Smith Elder in the beginning of September 1847; it came out in October and had the resounding success which has acclaimed it ever since. Why?

Jane Eyre

Partly, I think, because it is in a way the Cinderella story, beloved down the generations: poor girl suffers much, but eventually marries the Prince. Partly, also, because it has Charlotte's continual theme: a young person of integrity struggling to maintain that integrity in a harsh and cynical world. More and more this story becomes topical; look in any bus queue and you will see half a dozen young girls in the same situation, going to work. Partly because, quite simply, it is a thrilling tale.

Jane Eyre is not a particularly Yorkshire story. The horrid Aunt Reed and her brood, who bully poor little orphaned Jane so abominably, might live in some northern county or other, but we are not told which. The appalling Lowood school, founded on Charlotte's bitter recollections of the Clergy Daughters' School at Cowan Bridge in Westmoreland, whose severities of regime really killed her two elder sisters, Maria and Elizabeth — or at least set them on the road to consumption — lies near the Lake District, amid fine rolling hills, with a charming stream at the foot of the garden. When Jane emerges, advertises and secures a post as governess to Mr Rochester's ward, and comes to his house, Thornfield Hall, we are told this is seventy miles nearer to London than Cowan Bridge and near the large manufacturing town of Millcote, but the shire again is left anonymous. The coachman's answer to Jane, in Millcote, who asks how far is Thornfield, how long will it take to reach it, is "Happen an hour and a half". That *happen* has a Yorkshire turn, but Mrs Fairfax the housekeeper does not speak in Yorkshire, nor does Leah nor the mysterious Grace. Rochester and his friends are of the class which disdains dialect, Adele of course speaks French; the landscape is agreeably hilly but might be anywhere. Not until the climax has been reached, Rochester's living wife revealed, Jane's wedding broken, Rochester's appeal to stay with him and be his mistress refused, and Jane escaped from Thornfield, do we reach any indication of moorland — and then it is in Derbyshire. The moorland here is very accurately and attractively described; Ellen Nussey's brother had recently obtained a living in Hathersage, Ellen had stayed in the Parsonage there to prepare it for the return of her brother and his bride, and Charlotte had stayed with her. (There are Eyres buried in the graveyard too; suggestive.)

As for Rochester, what is one to say? A reader told me bluntly the other day that he thought little of the Brontës; I meant to remark that very few English-speaking persons do not know who and what Rochester and Jane Eyre are, but was interrupted. Rochester is the type of spinster's hero, I know, and Jane is the Cinderella. But what a Cinderella! Note how she responds to his first proposals:

> "Do you think, because I am poor, obscure, plain, and little, I am soulless and heartless? You are wrong! I have as much soul as you, and full as much heart! . . . My spirit addresses your spirit . . . as if we stood at God's feet, equal — as we are!"

The Irish and Cornish genes, and let us hope some part of the Yorkshire upbringing, have certainly produced a writer capable of creating a woman of spirit.

Wuthering Heights when published by Newby after many delays in December 1847 was not very well received by the reviewers, some of whom found its author "brutal and morose". As for the quiet, delicate *Agnes Grey* published with it in the same volume, very little notice was taken of it at all. But, says Charlotte cheerfully, her sisters were both prepared to try again. Whether Emily wrote any other fiction we do not know, none has remained to us. Anne however wrote *The Tenant of Wildfell Hall.* Charlotte thought its subject a complete mistake, but Anne believing it her duty to write about a drunkard in his home, worked steadily on. When the novel was finished to Charlotte's disappointment she sent it, not to Smith Elder, but to the (in Charlotte's view) horrid Newby, and they brought it out in July 1848. Meanwhile Charlotte, overjoyed, as who would not be, by the many fine reviews and splendid sales of *Jane Eyre*, and encouraged by her publishers, began joyously to write *Shirley*.

Shirley

But between chapters 23 and 24 terrible things happened. Branwell had now deteriorated to the point where a sheriff's officer came to the Parsonage door demanding that the young man should pay his debts or accompany him to prison;

The Black Bull, Haworth. The wayward Branwell used to frequent this hostelry which lies at the foot of the churchyard.

perhaps worse, the foolish boy actually wrote a note to his friend, John Brown, begging him to buy fivepennyworth of gin for Branwell:

> "Punctually (sic) at Half-past Nine in the morning you will be paid 5d. out of a shilling given to me then:"

A friend of his tells how he went to Haworth to see Branwell, but when Branwell came into the room at the *Black Bull*, he was such a ghastly object, a mass of unkempt red hair surrounding his yellow hollow-cheeked face, that his friend hardly recognised him.

In September Branwell still walked in the village; but then suddenly he was dying. (The story of him wishing to die standing up is not true.) Towards the last, his harsh expressions and seeming hatred towards his family faded, and he became the loving brother they had always known. On 27th September 1848 he died.

Emily caught cold at his funeral and with terrible rapidity seemed to hurry down the inexorable slope of tuberculosis towards death. The dreadful addition to her sisters' grief was that she refused all help, all medical attention, fed the dogs and performed household tasks as before, though soon she could hardly descend the staircase. Charlotte, to please her she hoped, sought on the moors till she found a late sprig of heather in bloom, and laid it beside her sister — who did not recognise it. On the morning of 19th December there was an obvious and alarming change in Emily: "if you will send for a doctor, I will see him now", she murmured. It was too late; in the afternoon she died. Her great dog, Keeper, walked beside Mr Brontë to the funeral.

She was hardly buried before it became all too clear that Anne, in the quiet but awful grief of having lost her dearly loved sister, was to follow the same fearful road. Anne, however, accepted doctors' instructions and followed them faithfully. Charlotte consulted advice in London, Mr Brontë in Leeds. Dear Anne had a great desire to go to Scarborough; she had visited this seaside resort with the Robinsons and laid the scene of Mr Weston's proposal to Agnes Grey there, so clearly the place had a special significance for her. Doctors advocated change of scene; Ellen Nussey gladly accepted the responsibility of accompanying her alone but neither Anne nor Charlotte could allow this.

At length in May Charlotte, Ellen and Anne went to

Scarborough. Anne had received a bequest of £200 from her godmother, and it was right she should use the money to buy something to please her. The travellers paused in York to buy bonnets and see the superb Minster; everyone helped them on their journey. They stayed in good rooms in Scarborough and saw a glorious sunset. Next day Anne drove in a donkey cart on the sands, characteristically taking the reins herself lest the donkey boy drove his steed too hard.

On the Sunday she wished to be taken to Church to participate in the public worship of God. But Charlotte dissuaded her. Next day, 24th May 1849, Anne died, quiet and serene, as dinner was announced at the door.

Charlotte hardly knew which she found worse to bear, she wrote to Smith Elder's chief assistant, Mr Williams, later: the calm Christian death of Anne, anticipating gladly as she did the entry to God's heaven, or the stern simple end of Emily, whose spirit seemed strong enough to bear her to fulness of years.

Charlotte finished *Shirley*, though with much less élan than she began it. No wonder that Chapter 24 is headed *The Valley of the Shadow of Death.*

"Calm your expectations, reader," Charlotte adjures us on her first page of the book. "Something real, cool and solid lies before you; something unromantic as Monday morning." She is right; but we can rejoice in it.

Shirley, Charlotte's third novel, is a completely Yorkshire tale. Its setting is Yorkshire: though the localities are called Nunnely, Stilbro' Moor and Fieldhead, they are drawn from the real Kirklees and Oakwell Hall and the district round Hartshead. Its story, an account of the Luddite rising in 1812, tells only of the Yorkshire part of this unrest; the attack on Hollow's Mill is derived from the real attack on Rawfolds Mill (in Liversedge, near Hartshead), and the shot fired at Robert Moore is taken from the (in fact murderous) shot fired on William Horsfall in the not far away Colne Valley. We must remember that not only the grounds of Roe Head, Miss Wooler's school, practically bordered the sloping hillside where the Luddites assembled, but also that at the time of the rising, Mr Brontë was curate at Hartshead, and lodged nearby in a house, Lousey Thorn Farm, which was not far from the *Shears* Inn, the local Luddites' headquarters. Mr Brontë knew the owner of the mill attacked. Mr Brontë and Miss Wooler, in very different ways, were both excellent raconteurs, and Charlotte heard often of the Luddites.

Who and why were the Luddites?

Part of the many processes of manufacturing cloth was the use of teazel heads to rough up, really to thicken and strengthen the fibre of the woven material; then the surface was "cropped", sheared to make it smooth again. Cropping, in which large heavy shears were used, was a highly skilled process, and the croppers were comparatively well paid. At the beginning of the nineteenth century a homely machine called a "frame" was invented in Lancashire, then adopted in Yorkshire, to do this cropping by the use of water-power. The croppers, faced by redundancy since one frame could do the work of ten men, resented the frames bitterly, banded themselves together in angry groups, smashed the frames as they were brought from their makers to the mills, attacked the mills and threatened to attack the millowners personally. To add to England's difficulties at this time, she was deep in the long war with Napoleon, who by his famous Orders had cut off much of the country's trade. All this is faithfully recorded, not without some impartiality, by Charlotte in *Shirley*, for as well as having personal reminiscences she also studied the accounts given in local newspapers.

The novel thus deals with outdoor events, and gives indeed a lively picture of vigorous, various, parish and provincial life. Apart from Mrs Gaskell's novel of Lancashire industrial life *Mary Barton*, written at the same time but published slightly earlier, *Shirley* is the first regional novel, and the first industrial novel, in English literature.

Naturally most of the characters in the tale are Yorkshire folk. There is Joe Scott for instance, Moore's foreman, who is left in bondage by the Luddites at the side of the moorland road, and when urged by Mr Yorke, who thinks he is drunk, to get up replies calmly that he can't "we're teed wi' a bit o' band." Joe knows very well the difference between "clean pride and mucky pride," and says proudly that "us manufacturing lads is a deal more intelligent nor th' farming folk in the south, we'se look after werseln."

The best of these Yorkshire people is, of course, the textile manufacturer, long established in that business, Hiram Yorke. Mr Yorke has travelled a good deal, can speak several languages — including excellent English — when he likes; but a

Yorkshirewoman cannot but feel some glee when one notices that the higher the rank of the person he addresses, the more Yorkshire his speech becomes.

Besides this external interest of Luddites, *Shirley* has another fine theme, which Charlotte knew from the inside, carried indeed for years in her heart. Caroline Helstone, the parson's niece, loves Robert Moore, the almost ruined, fiercely determined, half Belgian, half Yorkshire millowner. He seems not to love her, or rather perhaps to love her but be determined to marry for money—Caroline has none—to save his mill. Caroline is slowly, quietly breaking her heart for love, as Charlotte did, when the arrival of Shirley and Mrs Pryor saves her. It is a beautifully, delicately drawn study.

With the exception of Caroline, the characters in *Shirley* who are not Yorkshire are not, in my opinion, as well drawn as the natives. (I except from this dictum the Moores' Belgian sister, Hortense, whose self-righteous dealing with Caroline about darning and French poetry, and with her maid Sarah about soup and choucroute, is very funny indeed). In all Charlotte's four novels there is a master-pupil relationship between a man and the woman who loves him; in *Shirley* there are two. Robert Moore dominates Caroline, and Louis Moore has been the tutor and remains dominant over Shirley. Robert the manufacturer is thoroughly alive; Louis the tutor is not. Perhaps this is because his past association with Shirley is not told directly, but only in retrospect.

But perhaps, too, we must reflect that it is not Charlotte's fault that rich Victorian heiresses had nothing to do. Caroline laments this lack of occupation profoundly. Shirley herself is meant to be a portrait of Emily Brontë as she would have been if rich and free; and many fine, active women today have been given the name of Shirley by mothers who admire her. Shirley is meant to be "sister of the spotted, bright, quick fiery leopard" as she bounds into the Fieldhead parlour with her great dog Tartar at her side. But there is so little for Shirley to do! To send provisions to the soldiers defending Hollow's Mill, to engage in well-planned charity—administered, of course, by male clergymen—to read, to walk with Caroline, to supervise the distribution of milk. Emily, who did baking and cooking and supervised housecleaning and laundry and wrote books and poems, would have been bored to distraction by Shirley's empty life. One of the fine pieces in *Shirley* is indeed

Caroline's passionate plea for some occupation for the un-married girl.

We are grateful for delicate Caroline, for the attempt at Shirley, for hard Mr Helstone (so agreeable to silly women), for Mrs Pryor surely the most realistic long-lost mother ever portrayed, most of all for the picture of industrial Yorkshire — especially for Hiram Yorke and Joe Scott, who would serve admirably for pictures of people in similar positions, perhaps not today, but certainly up to twenty years ago. This is our county, we say, and if it is as unromantic as Monday morning, Monday has its moments too.

Villette

Charlotte then took two years to write *Villette*, being interrupted as she struggled on by illness in Mr Brontë, illness (of the liver) in herself, and the quiet but sad death of poor old Keeper, Emily's dog. She was doubtful and worried about the book, sought the opinions of George Smith and Mr Williams anxiously about the first two volumes, and when the receipt, as she calls it, for £500 arrived from Smith without an accompanying letter, she immediately fancied there was some disappointment about *Villette* and had not a note arrived from Smith on Monday would certainly have journeyed to London herself. But, as Mrs Gaskell tells us, when *Villette* appeared, it was received on publication "with one burst of acclamation".

The book is not at all Yorkshire, except perhaps in the character of the heroine, Lucy Snowe; its scene is completely Villette, i.e. Brussels. The reading public, who had at this date not seen or heard of *The Professor*, were almost stunned by the novelty of Madame Beck's boarding school for young ladies. Nobody had ever written of such a scene before. George Smith, who thought — not without reason — that Dr Grahm Bretton and his mother in the novel, were drawn from himself and his mother, felt uncomfortable, and Charlotte suspected this; as for Mme Beck and M. Paul Emanuel, Charlotte knew all too well that they were portraits — recreated, no doubt, but all too recognisable — of Mme and M. Heger. She was anxious, later, to prevent a French edition of the book from appearing, but this was impossible. The Hegers suffered a good deal from *Villette*, but took the matter with grave dignity; Charlotte's letters to M. Heger — "those letters!" cried Mrs Gaskell in horror, suppressing all but the calmest portions of them — were in the Heger possession, but they held them secret until after Charlotte's husband was dead, and then gave them, not sold them, to the British Museum. Charlotte's hatred of Mme Heger and her deep love for M. Heger, show clearly enough in the novel. But on the whole the Hegers, whose admirable descendants I have met in Brussels, come out of a difficult affair extremely well.

Villette is more complex in construction than any other Brontë novel. We are not told Lucy Snowe's early history, and this I think is a fault of construction, though if Charlotte had told it, yet another set of people might have had to be introduced, characterised, given feelings, and the tale is full enough of them already. We see Lucy, young and visiting happily with her well-to-do godmother, Mrs Bretton, meeting schoolboy Graham and — this is really skilful — little Paulina Home, a darling though rather maddening child, some of whose mannerisms may have come from Mrs Gaskell's own youngest little girl, Julia, whom Charlotte loved. Then there is a break, and when Lucy emerges again she is first nurse to a wearisome patient, and then alone, in poverty, homeless. We do not know what this disaster was, which shadowed her life and mood, and therefore we find it less easy to sympathise with her settled gloom. But Lucy, though ice externally, has fire within. She takes herself to Brussels, almost by chance becomes nursemaid to Madame Beck's children, then gradually by sheer merit rises to be a teacher and a trusted superior.

It has been pointed out that *Villette* holds three sets of lovers, each of whom loves twice. Lucy Snowe first loves Graham Bretton, who by a happy chance is the school's doctor, but then turns to Madame's cousin, the "impayable" Paul Emanuel, with his short black, bristling hair, his face like a sullen tiger, his sudden tempers, his immense goodness. George Smith did not much care for him, but all Charlotte's other readers love him dearly.

Then there is frivolous, pretty, amoral Ginevra, an English pupil at the school who attaches herself to Lucy; she loves — or enjoys the homage of — Dr Bretton at first, but presently turns to the worthless but aristocratic Count Alfred de Hamal.

Dr Graham Bretton at first is deceived by Ginevra's beauty, and wastes much heart, time and money on her, but presently turns to Paulina Home, now grown-up, with a Count for a father.

All these characters are kept "on the boil" as it were, by Charlotte with consummate skill; we suffer the anguish of unrequited love, which Charlotte knew so well, with all of them.

That Lucy's character has something of the Yorkshire obduracy in it must be conceded. It is not as easy to love her as it is to sympathise with Jane Eyre. Lucy writes frosty letters in reply to Dr Bretton, declines to give M. Paul a friendly forgiving word, likes amateur acting and *therefore* decides to give it up for ever. If one refuses the joys fate offers, one can hardly expect fate (or whatever) to continue to offer more. All the same *Villette* is a masterpiece.

Emma

I always wish that Charlotte had given Lucy a childhood such as befell Emma, the heroine of an unfinished novel, begun after her marriage, the fragment of which was eventually printed in 1860 in the *Cornhill Magazine*, preceded by an introduction from the pen of its then editor, W. H. Thackeray.

An apparently rich gentleman drives up to the door of a reputable girls' English boarding-school and deposits there his daughter, the child Matilda. The Misses Wilcox fuss over her and make a favourite of her because she is rich, only to find later that the address her father gave as his own does not exist, and his riches do not exist either. Miss Wilcox rages coarsely at Matilda; the child, agonised, falls to the ground.

Any gloom on Matilda's part, after such a beginning, could easily be forgiven and draw the readers' sympathy. Had Lucy Snowe an equally horrible childhood? We do not know.

Poems

Charlotte wrote a considerable amount of verse, but unfortunately it is only minor verse, not poetry. Most of it is Angrian, dealing with some of the many incidents of the Angrian story. She understands rhyme, and has some perception, though not very much, of emphasis and rhythm. Her prose is plain and convincing, and she is capable of such phrases as "that bright darling dream" for the Angrian world. But only once does she do herself justice in poetry. This is not, strangely enough, in the verses she wrote on the deaths of Emily and Anne; though her heart was in anguished torment, her verse then is cold and stiff. No; her best poem relates to the Angrian world, the all-embracing web and its decay.

"We wove a web in childhood
 A web of sunny air;
We dug a spring in infancy
 Of water pure and fair
. . . We are now grown up to riper age —
 Are they withered in the sod?
. . . Are they blighted, failed and faded
 Are they mouldered back to clay?"

Branwell: Prose and Poems

All readers of the Brontës' lives have, I believe, a very deep and real compassion for poor foolish Branwell, so much admired by his sisters in youth, so deplored in his twenties for rum and Mrs Robinson, dead with no achievement in his thirtieth year. But when I read the innumerable pages of his early works, written in tiny semi-print about the foundation of the dream world he shared with Charlotte, Great Glass Town, and later the kingdom of Angria, I cannot help feeling that his sisters, aunt and father were mistaken about his talents. His friends from Halifax, the Leylands, have told us that he had a great fluency of speech, which he expressed in beautiful English and a charming voice. This I believe; but when he came to writing he had the kind of eloquence I associate with minor politicians — the words flow on and on but they say little and are, to speak frankly, a dreadful bore. Compare his writing of this period and theme with Charlotte's of the same (only one year's difference) age and story, and I am sure you will agree that Charlotte had every qualification to become a novelist, and Branwell none, except the desire to become one.

Branwell had several agreeable talents in a minor degree. He played the organ for the local branch of Freemasons' Christmas festivities; he set up a studio in Bradford and painted some jejune but respectable portraits of his landlord, wife and niece (1838); he was tutor to a man's two sons in North Lancashire (1840); he acted as ticket collector at two small stations on the new Halifax to Manchester railway line (1840-41); he became tutor to the Robinsons' young son Edmund at Thorp Green (1843-45). At none of these was he successful. In Broughton by the Sea he drank. He went to London to become a painter, never presented his introductions and did not venture to enter the Royal Academy. We have guessed why from his account of the Angrian Wentworth's visit

The four children, including a crude self-portrait, by Branwell. This is a much poorer piece of work than the oil painting of his sisters. The girls in this picture are, from left to right, Anne, Charlotte and Emily Jane.
Brontë Parsonage Museum

to the capital; the foolish boy from "instinctive fear of ending his pleasure by approaching reality" kept feeding himself with "little squibs of rums". This is the Nemesis of the Daydream; the fear of and flight from reality. On the railway, Branwell's accounts were disorderly and he drank, though he was not accused of any dishonesty; from the Robinsons' he was dismissed with ignominy — what really happened there we shall never know, no doubt the tiresome Mrs Robinson played a bad part, though Branwell lied about a clause forbidding her to see him in her husband's Will, since no such clause existed.

But look at his account of the beginnings of the *Young Men* daydream. It omits all the interesting details of winter, Tabby, candle, invention of islands etc. given by Charlotte, dwelling instead on the various groups of soldiers Branwell owned, then plunges (of course) into an account of the *Twelves'* war with the Ashantees. Branwell loves to describe wars, revolutions, battles, or failing them political scenes.

He translates Latin well, for Mr Brontë taught him, and very occasionally he strikes out a sudden good line.

I have always wished that Branwell had given the title *The Wool is Rising* to a tale of real life, for it is such a suitable and suggestive title for a West Riding tale. He used it, however, for a story of the foundation of the kingdom of Angria, written in 1834.

He is only known to have attempted one novel of real life: *And the Weary Are at Rest*. He is said to have brought the manuscript of volume I to an arranged meeting for a friendly competition with his friend William Dearden, Joseph Bentley Leyland attending as judge between their productions. Branwell read some of his novel aloud — a curious hodge-podge of satire on Calvinist practices and love-scenes with the neglected wife, Mrs Thurston, and thus gave foundation to Dearden's belief (quite erroneous) that the tale was, in fact, *Wuthering Heights*.

Emily: Novel and Poems

In defending *Wuthering Heights* from attacks made upon it by contemporary critics, Charlotte in her preface to the new edition of the book in 1850 wrote:

> "With regard to the rusticity of *Wuthering Heights*, I admit the charge, for I feel the quality. It is rustic all through. It is moorish, and wild, and knotty as a root of heath. Nor was it natural that it should be otherwise; the author being herself a native and nursling of the moors. Doubtless had her lot been cast in a town, her writings, if she had written at all, would have possessed another character. Even had chance or taste led her to choose a similar subject, she would have treated it otherwise."

Charlotte is exactly and precisely right. It is a fascinating study to discover that not only the landscape and the weather, but the characters and story, the dialogue and even the narrative style, not to mention the philosophy, of *Wuthering Heights* is strongly affected by its author's being a native and nursling of the moors. But let us turn first to the tale.

The moorland quality of the landscape is obvious. Not for nothing do we all tramp and squelch through those extremely uncomfortable, sometimes rough, sometimes marshy, couple of miles of the moors above Haworth until at last we come in sight of Top Withens. As a farm house it is much decayed, and we feel, smaller than the building occupied by the Earnshaws. But its situation — its views of moorland and again moorland, rising and falling away emptily for miles; its north wind blowing over the edge, its row of stunted firs, blasted to one

The decayed shell of Top Withens. Although the old farmhouse bore no relationship to *Wuthering Heights*, the setting might well have led Emily to use it as her model.

side by the power of this incessant wind, its range of gaunt thorns all stretching similarly one way, its thick walls and narrow windows — yes, this strikes us as the place where the frightful Heathcliff story of love and hate might well have occurred. That the grotesque carving of crumbling griffins and shameless little boys, comes from a larger mansion, High Sunderland on the edge of a high, steep and windy hill outside Halifax near Law Hill, the school at which Emily taught, does not matter at all; when it still existed High Sunderland was quite as high and as windy as Top Withens and had a fine inscription carved in its façade which probably gave Emily the idea of the name and date for the Earnshaws. (I had perhaps better remark here that there is a division of opinion about the pronunciation of Wuthering. Some readers think we should say *Woothering*. I was brought up to Wuther, and cannot change now, the *oo* sound is too soft for my northern tongue).

It was Ellen Nussey who first suggested to Edward Morison Wimperis, artist commissioned by Messrs Smith Elder in 1872 to illustrate the Brontë novels, that Top Withens was the original of Wuthering Heights. This suggestion was for long accepted, and many pictures in many media have been faithfully produced. Of late, however, another suggestion has been strongly urged, namely that High Sunderland was itself the original from which Emily drew; its situation in a slight dip at the top of a very steep rocky hill seemed to correspond with that of the Heights, while Shibden Hall, an agreeable timbered mansion in a green valley, some miles away, corresponded in situation with that of Thrushcross Grange. Certainly both High Sunderland and Shibden Hall were within reasonably easy reach of Emily during her period of teaching at Law Hill. I know both the projected sites well, and I feel that when High Sunderland still existed it was as much too handsome, rich and aristocratic as Top Withens was too small for the Heights, while Shibden Hall is very old and elegant, but round the corner in another valley. It seems to me that what has happened is what usually happens in the mind of a really creative novelist, namely that the two real buildings have been melted, fused, to make a fictional identity which, while local and real seeming, leaves the writer free to impress upon it the details which imagination and the course of the story require.

The interior of the Heights is also very much that of a West Riding moorland farm, for example, Top Withens. The outside door opens straight with no intervening passage, into the family sitting-room, or "house" as they call it; the ceiling is not underdrawn, but rises open to the roof, furnished only with a rack supporting oatcakes and legs of beef, mutton and ham; ranks of high pewter and silver dishes tower on a vast oak dresser at one end; the fire—of wood, peat and coal—is immense, as usual in our county; the painted tea caddy stands on the mantelpiece.

Especially we notice, too, how the moorland weather pervades *Wuthering Heights*. No writer in English literature has presented English weather more exactly or more beautifully, than Emily Brontë, except perhaps Thomas Hardy. Emily has weather in every section of the novel—not in great heavy slabs of description, but in neat, short, intensely evocative phrases. The afternoon set in misty and cold; the earth was hard with a black frost; the snow began to drive thickly; a young man shakes the white flakes from his clothes; dark night coming down prematurely, sky and hills mingled in one bitter whirl of wind and suffocating snow; all day had been flooding

Pennine weather. A rain squall sweeps down the Calder Valley from the crest of the Pennines and the Lancashire border.

with rain; a swamp whose peaty moisture is said to answer all the purposes of embalming; the blast wailed by; the air now still and cold as impalpable ice; the whole hill-back was one billowy white ocean; a fine June day; a very dark evening for summer; the storm came rattling over the Heights in full fury; a bright frosty afternoon; soft thaw winds and warm sunshine and nearly melted snow; the weather broke; the summer shone in full prime; "I watched the moths fluttering among the heath and the harebells, listened to the soft wind breathing through the grass and wondered how anyone could ever imagine unquiet slumbers for the sleepers in that quiet earth."

The dialect spoken by that surly Yorkshireman Joseph, is, of course, completely that of Haworth neighbourhood. "All warks togither for gooid to them as is chozzen," says he to Catherine, and when asked to perform some small service for Heathcliff's unhappy wife Isabella, he retorts: "I getten summut else to do." Hareton Earnshaw replies to his new aunt Isabella in a jargon which, she says, "I did not comprehend". But a difference in speech between north and south, metropolitan and local, even in the gentry, is marked by Ellen Dean, who observed that Edgar Linton had a sweet, low manner of speaking and pronounced his words as Mr Lockwood does: "that's less gruff than we talk here, and softer." The blunt all too frank manner of Yorkshire conversation is well marked again by Ellen Dean when she observes that "we don't in general take to foreigners here, Mr Lockwood, unless they take to us first." Charlotte tells us that Emily did not mix with the Haworth natives — she certainly did not teach in the Sunday School and probably rarely entered their houses. "And yet," adds Charlotte with conviction; "she knew them". One of the great sources of local speech for a modern author was at one time the train, but is now the bus, where marvellous sardonic anecdotes, delightful vivid turns of phrase, can be heard at any time by those who listen. Emily had no local train or bus in which to eavesdrop. But she listened to her father's stories and to Tabitha's; perhaps — I think certainly — to Branwell's, for he knew the sexton and the local masons, who would abound in local intonation. Also, she heard the rough, loud, cheerful Yorkshire voices as she passed up and down Main Street; she talked, or at any rate listened, to the milk boy and the butcher and in any case spent more time in Haworth than any other Brontë. Her Yorkshire speech is perfect.

Of one other point, we may be certain. The story and the character of Heathcliff were probably planted in Emily's mind during her sojourn at Law Hill, for a great deal of the story and the character existed, so to speak, in the next field and still

Here at the top of Main Street, Haworth, *The Black Bull* stands much as it did when Branwell Brontë frequented it during his lifetime.

remain recorded for us in the diary of Miss Caroline Walker, who played a minor part in it.

The Walkers were a respectable old family, farmers and manufacturers in the Halifax worsted industry. John Walker sent his elder son to the university where he lost the business touch; his younger son died. John adopted a nephew, a sister's son named Jack Sharp, who soon dominated the whole family, thrusting the real heir, John Walker the second, out of control. Presently, however, John the second married and had children, but even then the abominable Jack Sharp's influence was still powerful; he in his turn adopted a scamp of a nephew, and encouraged him to lead John the second's children into evil ways. This story, well known and no doubt much gossipped about throughout the Halifax area, shows exactly the same kind of transmutation as the landscapes of Wuthering Heights show to Top Withens; the bare bones are there, but Emily adds the jealousy and mutual hate of Hindley and Heathcliff; the raging passion of Heathcliff and Catherine, the minor but essential sub-plot of the Lintons, the redemption of Hareton. She makes, that is, from an incoherent old wives' tale, a work of art. Incidentally, the Walkers had an old Biddy in their kitchen whose lines are those of Ellen Dean.

Some readers find the story of *Wuthering Heights* involved and difficult, but its *dramatis personae* is clear and plain. The Earnshaws, an old Yorkshire farming family, have lived at Wuthering Heights since 1500. The family when the story begins consists of Mr and Mrs Earnshaw and their teenage children Hindley and Catherine. Mr Earnshaw walks to Liverpool (sixty miles) and back. This walk, for a man in middle age, used to strike me as improbable, but I was wrong. A continual traffic in Irish cattle landed in Liverpool in the old days (and indeed still lands in Wales); these animals were sometimes sent direct to the abattoirs in Lancashire or West Riding towns, sometimes were placed in local herds to be fattened for later beef. I have met records of their routes and the fields where they paused on their way, in both North and West Ridings. That relatives from farming families in our northern counties sometimes drifted into connections with Irish cattle-boats and Irish farmers is natural enough; natural, too, that farmers or butchers in the northern counties often had business to transact in Liverpool. The Earnshaws had no horses.

On the occasion Emily speaks of Mr Earnshaw in Liverpool saw a ragged, starving young Irish boy lost in the street, apparently homeless. This boy he brought home with him to Wuthering Heights. He and his wife had previously lost a son called Heathcliff; they gave this name — not coupled with any other — to the Irish waif. From this Heathcliff springs all the evil in the book. With wonderful subtle skill, in a series of small incidents, Emily indicates how this boy, without at first any actual intention, upsets every relationship in the Earnshaw family. Mr Earnshaw dotes on Heathcliff, therefore Hindley is bitterly jealous of him; Catherine, wilful and sparkling, loves Heathcliff with heart, soul and body; Mrs Earnshaw resents him as an interloper. (She is a rather shadowy figure, for Emily knew a mother only for three years). The Earnshaw parents die, Hindley, now master of the Heights, marries a delicate girl who soon dies, leaving him a son, Hareton. Hindley treats Heathcliff badly.

Lower down the valley in Thrushcross Grange which has a park, good green grass, fine tall trees, live Mr and Mrs Linton, rich gentry, with their two fair teenage children, Edgar and Isabella. Through a romp the four children meet, Catherine's ankle is bitten, the Lintons nurse her, tame her manners, reject Heathcliff. Catherine, false to her heart, persuades herself that marriage with Heathcliff would degrade her. Heathcliff runs away, Catherine marries Edgar. Three years later, Heathcliff turns up, rich, educated, with the manners of a gentleman. Catherine is delighted to see him, Edgar appalled; Isabella unfortunately falls into a false romanticism and loves him. Bent on revenge against Hindley and Edgar, Heathcliff elopes with Isabella and marries her. She has a son whom she calls Linton, but she escapes from her husband and lives in the South of England. Catherine in horror gives birth to a daughter Cathy, and dies. After Isabella's death Edgar fetches the delicate, fretful Linton Heathcliff to live at Thrushcross Grange, believing he will be a playmate for his own darling daughter Cathy.

Heathcliff, partly for revenge, partly to secure the Lintons' heritage for himself, entraps Cathy into marrying his son Linton. Heathcliff has brought up Hareton, the Earnshaw heir, to be brutal, illiterate and poverty-stricken. But now that his revenge is so near accomplishment, he loses his taste for it and thinks only of his dead love, Catherine. He is foiled by the next generation's capacity for simple human affection, for Cathy and Hareton marry and are happy together.

Here in *Wuthering Heights* we meet first Mr Lockwood, a stranger from the South who has rented Thrushcross Grange from Heathcliff. He has just returned from a visit to his landlord — he is ill received by Heathcliff, a set of ill-mannered dogs and a beautiful young woman, whose identity, maddeningly, he cannot for some time decipher. The snow descends, he has to stay the night and has an agonising experience, partly dream of the Catherine of the past, partly nightmare. When he at length is safe at home, the housekeeper Ellen Dean begins the long story of Heathcliff and the Earnshaws. Slowly, gradually but enthrallingly, the frightful tale emerges, in talk between Ellen and Catherine, related by Ellen; in narrative by Ellen of Heathcliff's departure and Edgar Linton's love for Catherine, of their marriage, of Heathcliff's sudden reappearance, of silly Isabella's infatuation with Heathcliff and elopement, told to Ellen by Isabella; the long tale of Heathcliff's trap for young Cathy, told partly by Cathy, partly to fretful Linton Heathcliff, partly by housekeeper Zillah. Then Ellen again, then Mr Lockwood.

This is a wild, fierce, startling but not confused or entangled tale. Only five main characters are involved, with three in the next generation. The feeling of anguished wondering what on earth is going to happen next comes from the way in which the story is told. The only other English novelist I know who tackles his story, mutilates his narrative, in this way, is Joseph Conrad, who similarly begins the tale of *Nostromo* practically at the end.

Is it mutilation or enhancement? Enhancement, I think. A very great increase of suspense in the reader.

Poems

Emily's poetry seems to me to arise from and take the form of the moorland environment she loved so well. It is bare, bleak, austere, unadorned — and superb. There is nothing pretty about it. The form is not experimental and one hardly notices its scansion. The words are not erudite nor unusual nor highly coloured; they are plain and ordinary. But the arrangement of the words, and the feeling which inspires them, is so powerful, that it is impossible to read them without emotion. Take for example this simple verse:

"Where the grey flocks in ferny glens are feeding" . . . Emily Brontë would find little change in this scene today.

> "The night is darkening round me,
> The wild winds coldly blow;
> But a tyrant spell has bound me
> And I cannot, cannot, go."

Read this to yourself, or aloud to an audience, and at once all hearers feel they are on a high bleak rock overlooking a rough mountain landscape, battered by strong winds without and ravaged by savage passions within.

In 1844 Emily copied out many of her poems, hitherto written here there and everywhere, sometimes even on old envelopes or scraps of notepaper, into two notebooks. One of these was headed: "Emily Jane Brontë, Transcribed February, 1844 / GONDAL POEMS." The other has no heading, so we are tempted to assume that while the first notebook was all Gondal, the second was full of subjective, personal pieces. Whether this was so or not, we at least know that the first notebook poems referred to Gondal, and are helped to remember the creation by Emily and Anne of their daydream world, which occupied them so long.

Gondal was an island, in the north Pacific (but with a climate very like that of Haworth) where wild winds blew and the sea was storm-tossed. It had a king, Julius, and (most important) a Queen (Rosina or Augusta Geraldine Almeda); it had also Royalists and Republicans, armies, prisons, battles, fierce love affairs; and Emily and Anne "played" (their word) at these imaginary creations when they were alone together. When they journeyed to York in 1845, for instance, they "were" — again Emily's word — "Ronald Macalagin, Henry Angora, Juliet Angusteena, Rosabella, Ella Egremont", escaping from the palaces of instruction. The Gondal characters, to some of whom Anne gave different names, were thought by Anne, as she says in this year's birthday note, to be "not in first-rate playing condition" but Emily says that "they still flourish, as bright as ever". Here is part of a Gondal poem by Emily, a farewell from Augusta to Julius:

"Cold in the earth, and fifteen wild Decembers
From those brown hills have melted into spring —
Faithful indeed is the spirit that remembers
Such years of change and suffering!"

An extremely fine piece of research on Gondal has been achieved by Miss Fannie Elizabeth Ratchford of the University of Texas, and she has arranged Emily's Gondal poems so as to form, or at least to indicate, a coherent account of the Gondal story in her volume *Gondal's Queen*.

A difficulty for modern readers is that we cannot know for certain which poems relate to Gondal, and which to Emily's own heart. To which do such superb poems belong as "No coward soul is mine", or "Well, some may hate and some may scorn?"

At one time the revulsion, anger and compassion in the latter were thought to enshrine Emily's feelings towards Branwell:

"Vain as thou wert, and weak as vain,
The slave of falsehood, pride and pain,
My heart has nought akin to thine —
Thy soul is powerless over mine."

But in 1839, as the poem is dated, and 1846, when it was first published, Branwell was still alive and not yet the failure he became.

For myself, I feel that the poem probably referred to Branwell and also to a faithless Gondalian. It is a habit of the creative mind to live through the events of real life, transfer them and remodel them to an imaginary image, write of them thus, and purge oneself of them in that way.

Many attempts have been made to fathom the mind of Emily Brontë. She has been called a mystic, but she was not religious in any ordinary sense of the word, for she says:

"Vain are the thousand creeds
That move men's hearts, unutterably vain,
Worthless as withered weeds
Or idlest froth amid the boundless main."

She has been credited with secret experiences of love — we do not know; there is no evidence either way. A recent attempt, by Professor Herbert Dingle, is interesting; his *The Mind of Emily Brontë* sets out to consider what kind of a mind could produce *Wuthering Heights* and Emily's poems. That her mind encompassed the universe, whole and small, so that she could write as a philosopher of the three wild desires which tear the heart of man, and of the grey flocks in ferny glens feeding, we can see for ourselves. That she had an all-embracing compassion coupled with a clear sense of good and evil, we see in *Wuthering Heights*; she understands, and portrays justly, the oppression and strength and evil in Heathcliff, the ignorance and brutality of Hindley Earnshaw, the weak gentility and kindness of Edgar Linton, the stupidity of Ellen Dean, the wildness and selfishness of Catherine. She understands, she portrays justly; she does not condemn.

This perhaps is the place to recount the fates of the Brontë poems, after Charlotte one autumn day in 1845 came across a notebook fully of Emily's poems. She was not, she tells us, surprised, because she knew that all the sisters wrote poetry. But she was astonished by the quality of the verses:

"I thought them condensed and terse, vigorous and genuine. To my ear, they had also a peculiar music — wild, melancholy, and elevating."

It was Charlotte who beat down Emily's reluctance to have her private world intruded upon, and when Anne mildly showed some verses of her own, insisted that the three sisters should jointly produce a volume. Emily was calmed to some degree by the veiling of their names: and the poems of Currer, Ellis and Acton Bell were published in 1846. Charlotte was the first, and for a long time the only, reader who appreciated Emily's superb cadences; let us give her thanks for making available to us some of the finest poems in the English language.

Anne: Novels and Poems

Anne's writings show less evidence of her being a native of Haworth than do her sisters'.

The settings of her novels are obviously not Haworth. Agnes Grey's first position as governess at Wellwood House has a background resembling Anne's at Blake Hall in Mirfield; while her stay with the Murrays at Horton Lodge is obviously based on the Robinsons at Thorp Green. These are landscapes very different from heathery Haworth. Scarborough is certainly Scarborough, castle and cliff just as she tells us when Mr Weston proposes to Agnes, and those delightful primroses on the lane bank beside Horton Lodge come straight from her moorland home.

Agnes Grey

Agnes Grey was praised by George Moore as a novel "simple and beautiful as a muslin dress"; and if one may add the epithet colourless, and deplore some of its unnecessary longueurs, one must agree. It has also an earnest sincerity, and at times an ironic penetration of human nature — especially of fond parents and foolish children — entirely admirable.

We do also gain from Anne in *Agnes Grey* a remarkable picture of what it was like to be the youngest of a family "in a lonely village parsonage among the hills". Agnes's father was a poor clergyman, her mother married him for love. Agnes had a kind, active, elder sister, who with her mother always regarded little Agnes as a *child* (Agnes's italics) and urged her not to try to help them in the work of the house, but play with her kitten or do a little easy plain sewing. No schooling, a few rare stately parties of elders as the only society. Agnes began to long to go out into the world, to see different people, to earn her living; in fact, to be a governess! Mother and sister Mary laughed when they heard this outrageous suggestion, Mr Grey laughed even more. For Anne, two years younger than Emily, four years younger than motherly Charlotte, with Aunt in the bedroom, was childhood life in Haworth Parsonage like this? I think so; for Anne is the most scrupulously accurate observer and recorder. She believes sternly in truth, and unlike the wilder Charlotte, found truth in honourable moderation. The most characteristic sentence in Anne's writing is: the one where she mentions a sitting cat's tail half encircling her velvet paws. *Half* encircling — that is the exact truth, and Anne records it.

With *The Tenant of Wildfell Hall* the case of Haworth is rather different.

The Tenant of Wildfell Hall

The home of the heroine of *The Tenant*, Helen, as a girl is chiefly in Staningley with her aunt in an unspecified county which is not Yorkshire, and partly in London; after her marriage she lives with her husband, Arthur Huntingdon, in another county which, though a good "shooting" county, is much nearer London than Yorkshire. The natives are not Yorkshire people and do not use the Yorkshire tongue. But the hero, Gilbert Markham, is a Yorkshire farmer, at Linden-Car, and Helen seeks refuge from her unfaithful and drunken husband in an old Elizabethan manor house a few miles away, called Wildfell Hall. Gilbert, going out one day in pursuit of destructive game-hawks and crows, walks up the hill to Wildfell. Anne's description of this walk, the changing country-side he sees as he goes is so exactly and accurately that of a typical West Riding hill that any Yorkshire reader recognises at once the accuracy of Anne's observation and presentation.

> "I left the more frequented regions, the wooded valleys, the cornfield and the meadow-lands, and proceeded to mount the steep acclivity of Wildfell, the wildest and loftiest eminence in our neighbourhood, where, as you ascend the hedges, as well as the trees, become scanty and stunted, the former . . . giving place to rough stone fences, the latter to larches and Scotch fir-trees, or isolated blackthorns. The fields . . . rough and stony, wholly unfit for the plough, were mostly devoted to the pasturing of sheep and cattle; the soil . . . thin and poor, bits of grey rock here and there . . . bilberry plants and heather — relics of more savage wildness, grew under the walls . . .
>
> Near the top of this hill stood Wildfell Hall . . . built of dark grey stone, behind it lay a few desolate fields . . ."

The stone fences, the larches and fir-trees, the stony fields, the bilberry plants and heather — they are all there still, just as she sees and portrays them.

Poems

To turn to Anne's poems: this is the place to tell fully of a trouble which befell the Brontës through the publication of the

Bell poems, for it concerns Anne and her character the most. Anne's second novel, *The Tenant of Wildfell Hall*, was published in December 1847 by Newby. *Jane Eyre* had appeared, and caused tremendous applause in October 1847. The abominable Newby evolved the idea of putting out a statement which implied that *Jane Eyre, Wuthering Heights* and *The Tenant* were all the work of one person. He endeavoured to sell *The Tenant* to American publishers on these lines. An American publisher who had already made an agreement with Smith Elder for the second novel by the writer of *Jane Eyre* wrote angrily to George Smith about what appeared a breach of faith on his part. Smith of course wrote to the Bells at the Parsonage.

To have their honesty impugned was something the Brontës could *not* stand. In anguish Charlotte and Anne took a decision — Emily, we are not told, but knowing her we can be sure — declined to accompany them. The others rushed through their housework, packed a little luggage, walked to Keighley in a thunderstorm — some authorities think this was a snowstorm, but the original letter to Mary Taylor is quite clear for thunder — took themselves to Leeds, caught the night express to London, went to the Chapter Coffee House because it was the only place they knew, and after breakfast found their way to the Cornhill premises asking for George Smith. At last they were ushered in to him; Charlotte, trembling but firm, silently proffered the letter he had recently written to Currer Bell.

"Where did you get this?" enquired Smith, staggered.

Charlotte explained that they were three sisters named Brontë, who had called themselves Bell, and denounced the ill faith of Newby.

Smith, excited by this revelation, turned up in the evening with two sisters all in full evening dress — it seemed they had come to take the Brontës to the opera! The Brontës put on the best clothes they had with them, and soon found themselves in the glittering scene of the Opera House. Charlotte was almost overcome, and resenting the condescending (and perhaps amused) glances of the richly attired women at the little old-fashioned provincials in their high necked dresses, whispered to George Smith: "You know, I am not accustomed to this sort of thing". But, she continues in her letter to Mary Taylor: "I glanced at Anne, and saw she was calm and gentle as always". How much this tells us about dear Anne! They went to church next morning, escorted by Mr Williams, dined twice with George Smith—both men were now their friends—and journeyed back to Haworth on Tuesday laden with presents of books, much goodwill, and as far as Charlotte was concerned, with sickness and headache.

Anne's poems show Anne as no more (but no less) than a conscientious and knowledgeable versifier, except when occasionally her deeper feelings spring into her rhymes. Her lament *Domestic Peace* shows how severely she felt Branwell's disrupting of it by his foolish conduct. A fine Gondal poem tells of her love for the winds and wilds of Haworth:

"That wind is from the North: I know it well;
No other breeze could have so wild a swell . . .
I have passed over thy own mountains dear,
The northern mountains, and they still are free;
Still lonely, wild, majestic, bleak and drear
And stern, and lovely, as they used to be."

And here is the poor child lamenting the loss of William Weightman, in terms which show how mistaken Charlotte was in considering their approach a mere light attraction:

"Yes, thou art gone! and never more
  Thy sunny smile shall gladden me;
But I may pass the old church door
  And pace the floor that covers thee.
May stand upon the cold, damp stone,
  And think that, frozen, lies below
The lightest heart that I have known,
  The kindest I shall ever know."

Her religious poems, on *The Narrow Way, I have gone backward in the work*, and the infinitely pathetic *Last Lines* reveal her sincere Christianity, her sad feeling of guilt, her earnest desire for self-improvement. My sister Anne, said Charlotte in her fine introduction to the 1850 reprint of *Wuthering Heights* and *Agnes Grey*, was well endowed with quiet virtues of her own: "long-suffering, self-denying, reflective and intelligent". The Christian virtues in which she firmly believed, supported her through her last, most painful journey when she died in Scarborough in her twenty-ninth year.

CHAPTER FOUR

Charlotte's Success

Smith Elder — Mr Williams — Sir James Kay-Shuttleworth —
London — Edinburgh — Harriet Martineau — Thackeray —
Mrs Gaskell

FOR a short time Charlotte enjoyed what might have been a brilliant success. Even in the West Riding, she says with amusement, she met sometimes with new deference and augmented kindness, while if ecclesiastical brows thundered at her because of those three Shirley curates, she did not care. She visited London twice, staying with the Smiths, attended Thackeray's lectures, went to tea with Harriet Martineau, saw Rachel act, visited the Great Exhibition at the Crystal Palace twice, the second time under the guidance of the distinguished scientist Sir David Brewster, and looked at the new Parliament Houses.

How did she fare in this society so new to her?

Not, I am sorry to say, very well. They viewed her with respect, even with veneration, but could not get into easy conversation with her. Thackeray, for instance — to whom the second edition of *Jane Eyre* had been dedicated — writes thus of her:

> 'I remember the trembling little frame, the little hands, the great honest eyes . . . New to the London world, she entered it with an independent, indomitable spirit of her own; and judged contemporaries . . . with extraordinary keenness of vision.'

But, says Charlotte: "with him I was painfully stupid."

There is an uncomfortable account of how Charlotte appeared at an evening party wearing a twisted band of silk round her head, for she had not enough hair of her own to form the plait then fashionable. Worst of all is the terrible description of the dinner party which Thackeray gave for her, to which he had invited critics and other literary persons. It proved, Thackeray's daughter, Lady Ritchie, tells us, a gloomy and silent evening. Everyone waited for the brilliant conversation which never began at all. Her father was too much perturbed to be able to cope with it. Straying into the hall for a little relief, to her surprise she saw Thackeray opening the front door with his hat on. He put his finger to his lips to assure her silence, walked out into the darkness and did not return. Another woman who met her on this visit wrote of:

"Miss Brontë's own inability to fall in with the easy badinage of the well-bred people with whom she found herself surrounded."

For this unease I am afraid Haworth was a good deal to blame.

Charlotte also at one time accompanied George Smith on a trip to Edinburgh with one of his sisters. Ellen Nussey had her own opinion of the relationship between Charlotte and Smith, and joked a little, amicably, about them as Jupiter and Venus. Charlotte rejected this firmly as nonsense, and Smith soon married a young and pretty girl. One notes, however, that he remarked on Charlotte's longing for beauty; he believed she would give all her genius and her fame to have been beautiful. This is perhaps rather an exaggeration; but when, many years later, Mrs Humphry Ward, well-known novelist who was preparing an introduction to the Brontë works, asked him for the truth of their friendship, he replied significantly:

"I was never in love with Charlotte Brontë, and I was not so conceited as to think she was in love with me, but I believe my mother was a little anxious at one time."

A visit which had more importance for Charlotte — and for us — than the London occasions, was made by her rather reluctantly, as the result of a call paid on the Parsonage by Sir James Kay-Shuttleworth (notable in medical and educational reforms) and his wife. They invited her to stay with them in their Lancashire home, Gawthorpe Hall, and later to the house they had built on the hillside above Lake Windermere, Briery Close. Here there suddenly entered the drawing-room, who but Mrs Gaskell! This noted novelist, married to a Unitarian minister in Manchester, who had several young daughters, observed Charlotte with a novelist's eye and ear. True, she wrote of her to a friend as a "little lady in black silk gown", but she mentioned also her "sweet voice", and noted that though Charlotte sometimes hesitated a good deal before speaking, when at last she uttered she used "admirable expressions". Luckily for us, Lady Kay-Shuttleworth had a bad cold and could not leave the house, so Charlotte and Mrs Gaskell boated on the lake together.

In a word, the two novelists became great friends. Thereafter they corresponded on intimate terms, and Charlotte actually visited the Gaskell home in Manchester. I cannot refrain from mentioning that Mrs Gaskell's youngest little girl, Julia, took a fancy to Charlotte and would sometimes wander up to her and put her small hand in Charlotte's. Julia sounds so like Paulina Home in *Villette*, which Charlotte began to write that autumn (1851) that one cannot but wonder whether some of the mannerisms of that deliciously drawn child were not created by — not of course directly drawn from — little Julia.

The previous autumn (1850) Charlotte had edited her sisters' novels and poems for a reissue by Smith Elder, and wrote the beautiful and pathetic biographical notice of Emily and Anne, with the separate preface for *Wuthering Heights*.

Mrs Gaskell's friendship, and some correspondence with Harriet Martineau, must have been a great pleasure and relief to Charlotte, now living alone with her father in the silent Parsonage. Mrs Gaskell, who stayed with her for a few days there, gives a detailed description of this silence, and records how after she had retired to bed she heard Charlotte's footfalls below, treading the dining-room — the lonely Charlotte still keeping up the custom she had observed with her sisters.

St Michael and All Angels Church, Haworth, as drawn by Mrs Gaskell in 1857. The Parsonage is to the left and behind lies the Sunday school.
Brontë Parsonage Museum

But Charlotte had for a little time a hope that her loneliness might be coming to an end. Ellen joked mildly about James Taylor, a member of the Smith Elder staff, "my diminutive and red-haired friend", as Charlotte calls him, and presently he is calling at the Parsonage, and it is clear from Charlotte's letters to Ellen that he had come to make a proposal. It can be seen, too, that Charlotte had serious thoughts of accepting him, but unfortunately as soon as he came near her "my veins ran ice", she told Ellen. She could not possibly accept him as her husband; everything has become complete bitterness and ashes, a more entire crumbling away of a seeming foundation of support and prospect of hope can hardly be imagined.

Papa falls ill; Charlotte goes to London and it is not a success; Charlotte falls ill with a liver complaint. She begins to write *Villette*, but takes two years to complete it. Her publishers grow tired of asking for her next novel and tend to allow subordinates to choose the gifts of books they send her; James Taylor is now in India; Charlotte is alone.

Was it a great grief, or a great release, to write about Paul Emanuel, who of course is drawn from M. Heger? We do not know. We do know that when *Villette* at last appeared, in 1853, it was greeted with one great burst of acclamation.

But Charlotte was still alone.

CHAPTER FIVE

The End of the Brontës

Deaths of Branwell — Emily — Anne — marriage of Charlotte

THE rest of Charlotte's life was in my opinion deeply sad.
For now Arthur Bell Nicholls comes fully on the scene.

One evening, when Mr Nicholls, as Mr Brontë's curate, had
been in the study discussing parish matters with Papa while
Charlotte as usual sat alone in the parlour, Mr Nicholls left,
and Charlotte expected to hear the front door of the house
close behind him. Instead she heard a quiet tap on the parlour
door. In a flash she guessed what might be going to happen.
Whether she had any real intimation we do not know — a
Bishop who had come to lunch a short time before said after
the event that he had guessed its approach; for ourselves, we
do not know. Mr Nicholls entered; the quiet man, in an agony
of distressed embarrassment, managed to utter a proposal of
marriage. Charlotte at once, with Victorian propriety, asked if
he had approached Papa; Mr Nicholls stammered that he had
not dared. Charlotte gently but firmly put him from the house,
promising a definite answer on the morrow. Then she went to
her father and told him what had happened.

Mr Brontë was furious, That his famous daughter, his only
remaining daughter, should marry at all was bad; that she
should marry an underpaid undistinguished curate seemed the
last insult. He commanded Charlotte to refuse, with so much
anger that she was alarmed lest some severe physical conse-
quence should ensue, and obeyed him.

A period of acute discomfort for all concerned followed. Mr
Nicholls gave in his resignation from the Haworth curacy; Papa
fumed; Mr Nicholls continued to take church services but
almost broke down during one of them, while all the women in
the congregation — who of course somehow knew everything —
sobbed around. Mr Nicholls left Haworth; he had thought of
going to Australia as a missionary, but instead came to a
parish at Kirk Heaton near Pontefract in Yorkshire. He wrote
to Charlotte. She had a fearful scene with Papa to obtain
permission to reply. Fortunately (perhaps) for her Mr Nicholls'

Patrick Brontë in old age.   *Brontë Parsonage Museum*

replacement as curate in Haworth was a Mr de Renzy, and he was not at all satisfactory. Thus, by such apparently unrelated trifles are crises sometimes decided. Charlotte and Mr Nicholls corresponded; he returned to Haworth, and soon Charlotte is writing to Ellen Nussey: "In fact, dear Ellen, I am engaged."

"I am still very calm, very inexpectant. What I taste of happiness is of the soberest order. I trust to love my husband . . . Providence offers me this destiny. Doubtless then it is the best for me."

This, from the woman who wrote of Jane Eyre and Rochester, Lucy Snowe and Paul Emanuel, seems to me unbearably sad.

They were married on 29th June, 1854, Miss Wooler acting the part of giving the bride away, as on the last night before the ceremony Mr Brontë announced that he did not mean to go to the church.

Some of the villagers had heard what was afoot, and clustered by the porch to see Charlotte pass. She looked like a snowdrop, they reported, in a white lace cloak, with green leaves in the white veil over her hair.

The Nicholls went to Ireland for the honeymoon, and Charlotte undoubtedly felt pleased to find the sincere regard and high social standing in which her husband and his family were held there. Unfortunately—for this may have been the cause of the later illness—when Charlotte was riding up the steep, beautiful pass through the Gap of Dunloe, her horse suddenly reared and plunged and she fell to the ground. Mrs Gaskell thought the marriage very happy, and we can allow ourselves to suppose so, for Charlotte spoke with real affection and gratitude of Arthur later. But she also wrote to Ellen:

"Indeed—indeed Nell—it is a solemn and strange and perilous thing for a woman to become a wife.

At least she was not now lonely; the little peat-cellar behind the parlour had been cleaned and decorated—Charlotte herself stitching the green and white curtains for its windows—and Mr Nicholls used it as his study, for of course Charlotte could not leave the Parsonage and Papa. Mr Nicholls took the services, and Charlotte rejoiced to have found such an able helper for her father.

All was well for a while, until one day Mr Nicholls with the best of intentions called to his wife to come for a walk. They set out happily across the moors, then decided to go on to the waterfall. Rain began while they were watching the water raging over the rocks white and beautiful, and they returned home under a stormy sky. Charlotte caught cold, and could not throw it off.

By January of the new year, 1855, she was continually attacked by sensations of nausea and faintness, and became almost unable to eat. During the autumn poor little Flossie, Anne's spaniel, had died; and now while Charlotte lay so ill, Tabby's health declined rapidly and she died. There was a natural cause for Charlotte's illness, for she was pregnant, but she was by now too weak to rejoice in the prospect of a child; she sank, and on 31st March 1855, she died.

Whether the Brontës' early deaths derived from tuberculosis, as has been widely accepted, for the bleak climate of Haworth gave this virus no remission; or whether Mr Brontë was himself a carrier of the disease; whether the appalling sanitation of the place contributed its quota; whether they derived their susceptibility from their mother; or whether some other cause operated; we really do not know. Modern medical opinion has expressed to me that Charlotte's death was due to *Hyperemesis gravidarum*, i.e. excessive sickness of pregnant women. I can't help feeling that Haworth had something to do with it, though not everything. In the West Riding we are apt to say jovially to each other on particularly sleety days: "You have to be tough to live here."

Mr Nicholls had been offered a good living in Lancashire, but of course he could not and would not accept it; Charlotte had trusted him to stay with Papa, and he stayed.

CURRER BELL IS DEAD, cried the newspapers, and many were the articles written upon her, in grief and commendation. But they abounded, as alas newspaper articles often do, in errors small or large. Even Harriet Martineau's otherwise fine tribute contains half a dozen mistakes, small in themselves, but irritating to bereaved father and husband. Mr Nicholls' wish was to say nothing and let the agitation die, but Mr Brontë found the accusations against himself and the virulent comments on poor Branwell quite intolerable, and wanted an answer made. Ellen Nussey, angry that her friend was insufficiently understood and commended, suggested that Mrs Gaskell should be asked to write a reply; Mr Brontë approved the idea of an account, long or short, of Charlotte's life and works. Mr Nicholls reluctantly yielded.

Mrs Gaskell was extremely conscientious about her task; she

Richmond's beautiful portrait of a beautiful woman, Mrs Gaskell.
National Portrait Gallery

visited every place Charlotte had visited, except, she says truthfully, "the two small private governess-ships". She went to Brussels; Mme Heger refused to see her, but M. Heger responded freely, showing her "those letters"; Mrs Gaskell felt a warm liking and respect for him. The Reverend Carus Wilson objected to the portrayal of himself and Cowan Bridge. Mrs Robinson also objected to the severe account written of herself. Her lawyers threatened an action, and Mr Gaskell had to write to *The Times* retracting all the details of that awkward story about Branwell. But in spite of Mrs Robinson, Mr Nicholls, and Ellen Nussey refusing to be mentioned in the *Life* as anything but E, the biography survived as one of the finest in the English language. It had a tremendous and continuing success when published by Smith Elder in 1857.

Meanwhile poor old Mr Brontë, having seen his wife and six children die before his eyes, lived on in the Parsonage with Mr Nicholls who, the villagers said, was apt to tyrannise over him. Mrs Gaskell took one of her daughters to see him; he was in bed, all in white of course, with white fluffy hair and rather pompous oratory. Mr Brontë had liked the *Life* at first, but later was vexed into turning against it; he forgave Mrs Gaskell now but gave her a carefully concealed warning to leave before Mr Nicholls returned.

In 1861 Mr Brontë died. Mr Nicholls went back to Ireland, renounced his clerical profession, became a farmer, married a cousin who had always loved him, kept a Brontë portrait and some of the daydream booklets for long years, till Clement Shorter came to visit him in 1895, and rescued them for us.

CHAPTER SIX

Haworth Today

The Brontë reputation today — Brontë Parsonage
Museum — books about the Brontës — modern Haworth

The Reputation of the Brontës To-day

WAS 1861 the end of the story of the Brontës? Well, no.
From the publication of Mrs Gaskell's *Life* until the
present year, there has been a continual stream of books and
later of plays, films, radio and television items dealing with
their lives. George Smith issued an illustrated edition of the
works in 1872-73. Copies of this edition, seven large volumes
including Mrs Gaskell's *Life*, were, to my great good fortune,
given by my father to my mother either in their engagement
days or shortly after their marriage in 1879, so that I (born,
may I mention in 1894), always grew up with them. Edmund
Morison Wimperis, a well-known watercolour painter and
wood-engraver of the day, consulted Ellen Nussey about the
locations named in the novels, and provided what George
Smith describes (and I thoroughly agree) as "clever and
characteristic sketches".

T. Wemyss Reid began the flow of Brontë studies with a
Charlotte Brontë Monograph in 1877; A. M. F. Robinson
followed in 1883 with *Emily Brontë*; Francis Leyland came out
with a book on the Brontë Family in 1886 with special
reference to Patrick Branwell Brontë; Clement Shorter's two
Brontë volumes 1896 and 1908 were for long the best account
available; now we have the five full *Shakespeare Head Brontë*
volumes; the splendid research of the daydreams by Fannie E.
Ratchford of Texas University; the admirable studies of each
Brontë by Winifred Gérin, and many, many more, for a new
generation of Brontë students is arising. In the midst of the
early Brontë interest Ellen Nussey complained bitterly that
she, the source of so much of the material which others used
(more than 400 letters) had received neither money nor glory;
she had been badly treated. This was true; but the poor lady
did not realise that it was largely her own fault for suppressing
herself into an initial for Mrs Gaskell. Ellen tried to get her
letters published, decided to print her own edition. They were
actually in print with a local printer when she discovered that,
Charlotte's Will having left all her property absolutely and

entirely to her husband, Mr Nicholls owned the copyright of the letters and they could not be published without his consent, which he certainly would not give. A letter from a Dorchester rector tells how, his wife being a friend of Ellen's, he himself burned or pulped the printed copies of the precious letters, retaining three printed copies for himself. Ellen too retained a few of these; where are they now?

A new development shortly arose which gave rise to great things for in December 1893 the Brontë Society was founded by a few Brontë enthusiasts. They formed it with the express purpose of keeping alive these famous Yorkshire authoresses, to emulate their virtues and to encourage others. They secured two rooms above the premises of the Yorkshire Penny Bank (as it was then called; now its title, more dignified but less welcoming, is Yorkshire Bank) at the top of Main Street, and collected many books, drawings, letters, personal relics and furniture from the Parsonage, to furnish these rooms as a Museum.

This Museum was opened on 18th May, 1895 with a good deal of ceremony. The railway had reached Haworth in 1867; several ordinary trains, and one special train arrived, "well freighted", says the official account. On emerging from the station the passengers were met, to their surprise, by the Haworth Brass Band, which escorted them up the hill to the Museum, and played in Main Street during the afternoon. In the absence due to illness of Sir T. Wemyss Reid, the opening ceremony was fittingly performed by Alderman John Brigg of Kildwick Hall, the Chairman of the Brontë Committee, in the presence of a crowd of several hundred people from many different localities. Sir T. W. Reid's address was read for him; among other suitable observations it contained the remark "the years of neglected obscurity which fell to the lot of the Brontës when they lived amongst us have been atoned for by the glory which now surrounds their name." Perhaps. A stained glass window placed in the church in 1884 bears the inscription, "To the Glory of God in pleasant memory of Charlotte Brontë, By an American citizen."

Brass tablets indicate the burying place of Charlotte and Emily; a large white tablet records the deaths of Maria and her six children.

The Brontë Society members were not satisfied with their two modest rooms, which indeed soon proved too small for the numbers who visited them. They longed to acquire the Parsonage as the proper home for the Brontë Museum.

In 1927 the opportunity presented itself of acquiring the Parsonage. Sir James Roberts — a native of Haworth who actually knew the Brontës, saw Papa and heard him preach, remembered Mr Nicholls and Charlotte's "frail unforgettable figure", indeed was actually born in Haworth during the week of Branwell's death — with his wife provided the funds for erecting a new Rectory, thus enabling the Ecclesiastical Commissioners to dispose of the old Parsonage. On 4th August, 1928, the title deeds of the old Haworth Parsonage were officially handed over by Sir James Roberts to Lord Brotherton, the then President of the Brontë Society, and thus

The Parsonage Museum sign, a metal silhouette silhouetted against the sky.

it became a permanent and national museum, entitled Brontë Parsonage Museum.

Very many manuscripts and interesting personal relics have accrued to the museum, and still do so. But the most important came from an American citizen, Mr Henry H. Bonnell of Philadelphia, who in January 1929 presented on loan (to be bequeathed at his death, which has since occurred) his collection of Brontëana, which included those fine examples of the tiny daydream booklets, so revealing, so rare, we can now see in the Bonnell room, carefully protected in a glass case.

The Brontë Society has found it necessary to build a neat addition to the back of the Parsonage to accommodate a resident curator, and to put up certain ropes and signs for the guidance of visitors. This is sad to those of us who preferred the Parsonage as little altered as possible, but when it is realised that in 1976 — last year alone — 189,220 persons entered the Brontë Parsonage Museum, the necessity for some guidance may be understood.

Only one object has ever been stolen from the museum, it was Keeper's dog-collar, which a few days later was returned by post.

Claude Meeker, journalist and United States consul in Bradford, unable to attend the opening of the first two-room museum in 1895, sent an interesting letter to represent him, in the course of which he remarked that "neither Charlotte Brontë nor her sisters have a memorial in bronze or marble." I mention this because it is now happily untrue. Since 1951 Miss Jocelyn Horner's fine bronze group of the three sisters stands in the exit hall in the Brontë Parsonage Museum.

Patient pilgrims of all ages queue to visit the Parsonage Museum.

THE BRONTE SISTERS

CHARLOTTE   EMILY   ANNE

This bronze group which stands in the Museum annex encapsulates the very essence of the three sisters. It is the work of the late Jocelyn Horner, and was praised by Sir Jacob Epstein.   *Brontë Parsonage Museum*

Modern Haworth

The village of Haworth, as it stands today, may be conveniently examined in three parts.

Firstly, there is the solid old core, perched on a hillside overlooking Bridgehouse Beck. Most of the grey housing that one sees on the ascent of Main Street was there when the Brontës were in residence at the Parsonage.

The Church of course has been renewed. The foundation stone of the present structure was laid on Christmas Day 1879 and the new building consecrated on 22nd February, 1881. Only the lower part of the old tower remains from the time of the Brontës.

But if the Church of St Michael and All Angels was not a contemporary of the Brontës, the Parsonage certainly is. Some alterations have been made during the intervening years and the kitchen has been largely remodelled.

Even the gaunt, rook-haunted elms that tower over the petrified forest of gravestones were planted by the Reverend Patrick Brontë's successor, John Wade. These trees have outstripped the Scots pines planted by Charlotte Brontë at the eastern extremity of the Parsonage garden.

The Bridgehouse Beck, widened here to form a mill dam, mirrors one of the textile mills already mature in years, but undoubtedly post-Brontë.

View of Haworth church from Aunt Branwell's room in the Parsonage. Only the lower part of the tower belongs to the Brontë's time. The Scots pine trees in the photograph were planted by Charlotte but the elm trees are younger.

Doubtless the family would still recognise much of higher Haworth even today but would have to acknowledge a change. Proper sewage dispersal and adequate water supplies; street lights; yellow lines at the curbs and a proliferation of traffic signs, to say nothing of a multiplicity of shop fronts, many of them proclaiming the name of Brontë, would evoke surprise. Poor Branwell would have to make do with a book or postcard were he to go to the shop which traditionally sold him opium; long ago it became a bookshop.

But there is still the odd corner where one can almost shut out the frenetic clamour of the twentieth century, with still the possibility of a carefully chosen view, framed by smoke-blackened stonework, of the cradling hills. Yes, there is grime on these stones, but then the gritstone of West Yorkshire can adopt this badge of honest toil with a dignity denied to brick. Or at least, as a West Yorkshireman I like to think so!

Below the old village, lining the Bridgehouse Beck, is the mushroom growth of Haworth of the Industrial Revolution, and the railway. Keenly interested though the Brontë girls were in the modern world about them (they each held certain railway shares) they never lived to see this form of transport became a reality in their village.

In this shop (then a chemist's) Branwell used to buy the drugs that contributed to his eventual downfall.

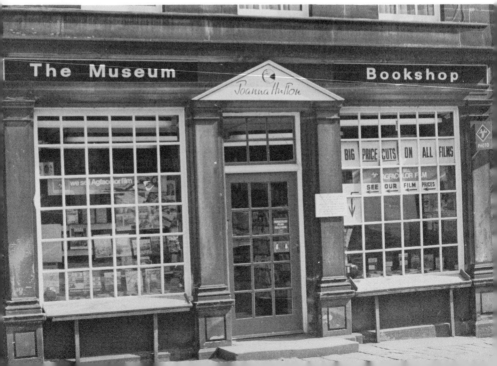

The engine sheds and sidings at Haworth station. This was not here in the Brontë's time but the sisters had some interest and shares in railway companies.

Three years before Emily's death plans were examined to carry a link from Hebden Bridge to the south. At that point the Transpennine railway came its closest to Haworth. And indeed just a few miles down the track, first at Sowerby Bridge and then at Luddenden Foot, Branwell Brontë worked as a clerk.

The dreams came to nothing and it was not until twenty-two years later that the noise of steam engines reverberated through the valleys of the river Worth and the Bridgehouse Beck. And even then the line did not connect with Hebden Bridge but only with Keighley.

It took from October 1861 to April 1867 to promote and build the five mile track to Oxenhope. For ninety-five years the line served the district before being finally axed by British Rail in 1962. And there the matter might have finished if it were not for a devoted band of enthusiasts who, accepting no obstacles, developed a privately owned railway that rivals the museum as a crowd-puller throughout the summer.

The Keighley and Worth Valley Railway Preservation Society was determined not to own simply a static museum piece. The

97

line is run as a viable commercial transport venture and is an excellent way to visit Haworth from the direction of the Aire Valley. One problem to be kept in mind however is the fact that Haworth station lies at the foot of a formidable hill while the other area of pilgrimage stands virtually on its summit.

Other vehicular traffic is able to mount the hillside though the volume over the years has far outstripped the ancient street's ability to cope. The problems of negotiating the roads jammed with pedestrians and oncoming traffic caused chaos at times and the need for parking spaces compounded the confusion. It was for that reason that in 1975 a new by-pass road was opened that skirts the village, taking all the down-going traffic away from Main Street.

In the main holiday season the large volume of private cars and excursion coaches swells the number of service buses that connect the village with Bradford and Silsden. For this reason land to the north of the Parsonage Museum has been cleared and a car park built.

The third face of Haworth would indeed cause comment among the Brontës. New commuter style housing, often of brick and in the modern style, makes use of the village fringes that would have been farmland during the last century—and until well into this century in many cases. Like many of the

Part of modern Haworth. Commuter housing on a street bearing a familiar name.

older streets that have been renamed in honour of the Brontë family and their works, they show pride in the heritage of the community.

But if roads and houses can show change and development within the village it is still possible to bridge the gulf of time.

Go out of season along the rough trackways over the ever brooding moors beyond. Just before I wrote these lines that is exactly what I did.

On a crisp, bright day in March with the sharp dry wind whistling and rattling through the sere stalks of the bent and wiry tufts of heather I retraced Charlotte's last outdoor excursion up the Sladen Beck to the Falls and Bridge. The erstwhile quagmire of the farm track was crisp beneath my feet and the mercurial play of light and shade from the cloud-scattered azure sky added an exciting sparkle to the air unique to the Pennine uplands. Sheep, mobile facsimiles of the lichen-covered boulders, unhurriedly browsed across the swell of the moors.

At that moment I was one across the chasm of time with those wild and noble minds whose owners wandered where I wander now, and saw what I see now. As I read their works I know that the spirit that motivated them and their masterpieces still roams this wild and lonely land.

In an early spring mist the Sladen Beck tumbles under Brontë Bridge. It is rare for a sheep to have this spot to itself.

The Brontë Falls are really some two hundred yards of boulder strewn hillside, over which a tiny stream discharges into the Sladen Beck. Most of the time it is little more than a trickle and here it is iced up in the grip of winter.

Index